The Rollercoaster

Julia Masters was born in England and has lived in Australia from the age of four. She was educated at Walford School and at Adelaide University where she received an Honours Degree in French language. She travelled widely and taught foreign languages then returned to university to study Law. She briefly pursued a legal career before taking up farming and writing. She and her husband live on a property in the south-east of South Australia, producing merino and cross-bred wool, prime lambs and beef cattle. She enjoys travel, gardening and spending time at the coast.

Five years of Julia's life were spent in infertility treatment, and this book spans the years from the Masters' marriage to the end of their involvement with the in-vitro fertilisation program.

the
rollercoaster

Julia Masters

**Wakefield
Press**

Wakefield Press
17 Rundle Street
Kent Town
South Australia 5067

Designed by Liz Nicholson, design BITE
Typeset by Clinton Ellicott, Wakefield Press
Printed and bound by Hyde Park Press

National Library of Australia
Cataloguing-in-publication entry

Masters, Julia.
The rollercoaster: a country couple's ride with IVF.

ISBN 1 86254 485 9.

1. Fertilization in vitro, Human – Australia – Case studies.
I. Title. II. Title: The rollercoaster: a country couple's ride
with in vitro fertilisation.

618.17805909

For the Wood family, and Lester

Author's note

Amanda Ryder deserves a great deal of credit for this book, as she believed that it should be published, working hard to that end.

Anne and Richard Clarkson gave great support, and while they provided the framework for encounters with Liz and Matt, these characters are entirely fictional, a composite of reactions that IVF patients might expect from others. The fictional dialogue shows nothing of the friendship and understanding the Clarksons gave us.

I would like to thank Michael Bollen for his skilled editing of the book and staff at Wakefield Press for their patience.

An enormous thank you to Mum and Dad. Fancy having to appear in a book as well!

Thank you, Lester, for not hindering the telling of what is also your story (but you and I know where the fig leaves are!).

Chapter One

I felt no pressure in the day ahead, but anticipated it with pleasure. Magpies chortled, with no sound of traffic to drown them out. I lay, relaxed, listening to Lester in the kitchen as he made a cup of tea. He brought it to me with a kiss and a silky terrier, damp from his first foray onto the lawn.

I sat up, raised knees helping to hold the covers around my shoulders, as I assessed the morning. Our bedroom, our bed, faced east, and I never drew the curtains on that window. There was no one out there to see us. Our home block ended two hundred metres away, and then there was a neighbour's forty-hectare paddock, rarely visited and with no buildings on it. It was his paddock, but our view — I hoped that he would never build there for any of his burgeoning family. Now it was populated only by huge river redgums, gnarled into fascinating shapes and graceful parabolas and to each of which it was easy to endow an individual personality. The night before I had lain in bed and watched the full moon rise behind the gums, making their white trunks gleam. I had seen twelve of the moon's performances here, and had already calculated that I hoped to see at least six hundred more. For now, in virtually the same position, it was the sun's turn to show what it could do, and it sprang into round red glory, fighting to burst through its cover of morning mist, colouring the trunks and clouds galah-pink.

'What is it they say? A red sunrise warns shepherds?' inquired my essentially prosaic husband. I looked at him not knowing whether to believe what I had just heard. My mouth twitched as I tried not to laugh at Lester, but his command of words was too striking, and I had to bend my head to my knees to hide my face as I giggled. Lester did not mind. Being a source of amusement to your new wife was a lovely way to start the day.

'Red sky at night, shepherd's delight; red sky at morning, shepherds take warning,' I corrected him, although he'd managed for many years in his ignorance.

'Aha. In any case, I'll be pleased if we get a decent rain.'

'It could be the early break to the season?'

'Yes, but on the other hand, if we only get a few points it could shoot the seed and then it'll all just burn. Plenty of hot weather to come yet.'

It was early April. The farm was in a high rainfall area, with underground water available too, but farmers always waited anxiously for 'the break', which was generally to be expected around Anzac Day. It was a good area—lush, green, divided into small but prosperous and well-kept farms.

I sat sipping my tea. Because the outside light was dim I was reflected in the bedroom window so that I was looking at the view through my own image. My appearance had already changed since coming here: I was slimmer, fitter, more tanned and my light brown hair had lightened further in the sun. My face had smoothed and lost the tired look that it had carried in the city. I shifted slightly so that I could see Lester and give him a mirrored grin. There he was: his broad frame and round balmy face under thinning grey hair. He winked at me.

We had married in March the year before, and I felt that I was now an experienced farmer as I commenced my second year of rural life. On a mixed grazing property such as ours—we run beef cattle, merino ewes and crossbred ewes—the months provide a constant variety of work, and I would not have felt right claiming to have finished my apprenticeship until I had seen the full range of tasks that each season brought. Now I felt able to handle anything, and looked back with amusement at my naivety of this time last year.

'Plans for the day?' I prompted Lester.

'You can go round the Hill ewes, if you like,' he replied, using the title we had given to a paddock and to the stock within it. Each year one mob of ewes, the oldest, were lambed early and then sold. This increased the length of the lambing season and therefore the availability of lambs for sale. Wool and beef were depressed, lambs were 'up'. 'I want to bring back a mob of hoggets from the other block on the truck and crutch them this afternoon. You can sweep the wool away for me while I crutch.'

'How many hoggets? How many truckloads?'

'Two, at least.'

'Good.' That would take Lester most of the morning, so I would be able to get some cooking done after checking the ewes while I waited for his return.

Checking a mob of lambing ewes involves driving amongst the mob, achieving a balance of not disturbing ewes that have already borne their lambs, and examining from a distance of a few metres if possible those that have not. Some of these may be having trouble giving birth, which will usually be obvious because part of the lamb will be showing but the ewe will be walking around non-chalantly as though she has abandoned all efforts to squeeze the rest of it out. Such a ewe has to be caught with the help of a dog, the lamb 'taken' – pulled out – and the two penned up together to give the ewe a chance to accept the lamb.

I did not expect to find any trouble, but took my favourite working dog, Laddie, anyway, as well as the pet silky, Murray. The clouds were dispersing by the time I arrived at the Hill paddock. It looked as though the season break would take a while to arrive yet.

I located the mob of sheep quickly and all was well, with lambs galore. But the mob should have been bigger, so I thought that I had better drive behind the hill and find any recalcitrants.

This was my favourite paddock. While all the others were flat and exposed, the Hill held the only remnants of scrub on the property, attracting emus and kangaroos. Behind its rise was a flat area bordered by a wooded laneway between ours and a neighbour's property. The laneway, the rise and a stand of gums formed the extremities of a grassy arena, private, quiet and special.

There hid the rest of the ewes, and in circling them I found one in trouble. The head of her lamb was out, its nose and tongue swollen as it tried to breathe. What a dilemma: because Lester was in the truck, which unlike the ute had no UHF radio, I could not call him to come and help. I would have to take the lamb myself, even though it was probably dead judging by the look of it. At least I wouldn't have to worry about where to pen the ewe and lamb up together, and I could save the ewe.

The question was whether to catch the ewe on foot, or in the ute. I observed it for a moment and saw that it was hobbling. The dog and I could run it down on foot.

'Laddie.' Good dogs waste no time wondering which ewe the boss wants caught, and Laddie headed straight for it. He ran for about fifty metres, wrestling with it, losing it, then eventually taking a firm grip on its shoulder, giving me a chance to catch up and straddle the ewe, one hand beneath its jaw and the other on its rump.

'Good boy, Lad. That'll do. That'll do!' The dog reluctantly let go of his prize and I addressed myself to the captive. 'You poor girl. What a trial to have to put you through—you're in a bad way anyway.' I caressed the ewe on the nose, then jerked it over so that it lay on its side. 'But I'm here to help you, believe it or not. I can't promise to do much for your baby, though.' I placed my knee on the ewe's side to hold it, found the lamb's front feet and pulled hard until it slithered out. It was a whopper. No wonder it had stuck. I poked one finger in its mouth to clear away the muck and miraculously the lamb spluttered and breathed.

'Hey, hey! Whacko! You're all right! Your baby's all right, Mum!' I slapped the lamb's side and encouraged it to breathe again, chuffed to have saved two lives. If I had not found the ewe, or if I simply abandoned it, foxes and crows would have finished it off. I had always associated crows and their haunting cries with country camping trips when I was a city girl, but now I hated them after seeing what they could do to the faces of weak stock.

I was again faced with a dilemma. The ewe and lamb had to be transported. If I were to let go of the ewe and head for the ute, the ewe would up and transport herself from this terrifying dog-filled scene, and consequently from her lamb. She needed immobilising. In the ute was a wonderfully effective immobiliser: a natty set of 'sheep handcuffs,' which gripped three legs of the sheep in a circle of metal with a clasp. But the ute was fifty metres away. Laddie was a clever dog, but he was not so clever that he could be sent to fetch an article. Not without seeing a picture of it first, I thought ridiculously, and the pen and scrap paper were in the ute.

I looked at the ewe, who looked up at me. 'You've got me stymied, Mum.' I considered my own person. 'I've got a hanky, I've got short socks … I've got a belt!' I took off my belt, wrapped it tightly around the ewe's front legs, added a back leg and tied the belt, then stood back. The ewe gave a struggle and realised that she was caught, then stopped. 'Gotcha!' I walked back to the ute, where Murray was shut in the cab yapping in excitement at the scene.

I soon lifted the lamb into the tray, handcuffed the ewe, rolled her up the tailgate and put the belt back where it belonged. The shearing-shed would be the best place to pen mother and child together, so I turned the ute to head back that way.

And, very shortly, stopped it again. Here was my favourite view, and if I couldn't admire it for a few minutes now, when I was my own boss and nothing urgent was waiting to be done, then when could I? Certainly in all my city jobs there would have been neither time nor opportunity to do this, and I said a quick thank you, to anybody who was listening, for my arrival here. Truly, my cup was running over. I stood leaning on the driver's side door of the ute, looking at the multiple shades of green where the stringy-barks, kangaroo paws and bracken fern grew in glades, and marvelled at my new job. I had always wanted to be a farmer, always, even through other changes of career, and here I was, achieving my dream early in life.

It constantly struck me that I was blessed, too, with the opportunity to live that dream accompanied by a loving, funny, romantic, quaint, responsible, old-fashioned man. I valued as well as loved him, could not quite believe that there was never going to be a time when he would play manipulating games. It was as though he had stepped out of an earlier time, values intact, true and totally trustworthy.

I couldn't even claim to have waited patiently for all this to happen. No, I'd always wanted it all yesterday, wanted to run before I could walk, my family would say, and had lived accordingly and tried to make dreams happen. And now my job was to drive through this beautiful setting, look after animals, and then spend the rest of the day with a soulmate. Incredible. Heaven forbid that I should ever take it all for granted.

After settling the ewe and lamb in at the shed I returned to the house, changed my clothes and began to cook casseroles to store in the freezer. I had learned the year before to have some main meals on hand for the days when I would have to do farm work all day long. I worked at my new timber island bench, the sort that I had always wanted.

This was paid for, as was the house and farm. It had been passed to the son whose hard work since age fifteen had helped to hold it. There were twenty hectares around the house, six hundred hectares in the main block just along the road, and one hundred and twenty hectares a short drive away that Lester had purchased before our marriage.

I was thankful that our situation was not so fortunate that I could spend without thinking, or that all the farm work could be done by paid labour. Lester and I had to budget, plan and co-operate, even if we didn't have to skimp. But it was in my nature to work, not to spend all my time shopping and socialising as some of the rich graziers' wives seemed to do. I had leapt at the chance to be a partner on the farm, and had made one stipulation: that I be a working partner in every sense. Lester had really encouraged that, teaching me constantly. It would be a new challenge as well as another change of career, and being self-employed in business would suit me.

I was glad that we had every incentive to work hard. There was much that we wanted to do together. Raise children, of course, God willing. Not a big family, just a manageable pair, and then we'd be free to make other plans. Lester was talking about building a weekender at the coast nearby. He also talked about expanding the farm, should a neighbouring block become available. A caravan – we loved touring – the further the better. New furniture. A new tractor and a trailer for the truck. Travel and more travel – we were both itching for it. It was good that while the future held challenges and hopes, the present was already prosperous. It would be easy for us, financially, to support a child or two.

Now that the stew was simmering I went out to the garden to pick some fresh herbs. Being at home for part of the working day was a treat and it seemed a wonderful notion that being a farmer meant never having to ask: Do I give up work to raise a child? When we had a baby I would adjust my farm duties but would be no less a partner on the farm, and would be able to ease myself back into those duties as and when I was ready.

Lester and I had decided that at least a year would belong to the two of us alone before we would think about children. Neither of us had been married before and we each wanted to savour marriage before we bit off parenthood. The year's delay had been a good idea. Lester had his share of adjusting to do, as after thirty years of independence on the farm he had needed to make room for a wife who was not used to giving way. Elements within each of us had clashed in the early days and taken time to amalgamate. I had to adjust to missing friends and my family in the city. I was just beginning to get to know some of the locals. Lester had to radically re-organise his time and work pattern: until marriage his life had been dominated by work but he recognised that he should try to strike a balance between dedication to the farm and relaxing with me.

Some of Lester's friends, however, were obviously not accustomed to a lengthy postponement of procreation. No sooner were we back from our honeymoon, it seemed, than we had been presented with a pram, playpen, clothes and sundries that had been used by various babies over recent years. I had uttered a few words of thanks, bitten my tongue, stowed the items in a spare room and shut the door. But lately I had been taking an occasional look at them.

The playpen needed painting, and the pram was not the modern sort that would fold up easily into the car for shopping trips. But if this beachhouse idea came to fruition I could leave the pram there and enjoy pushing the baby around the seaside streets.

Four tubs of casserole stood cooling on the island when Lester pulled up in the truck. I heard him washing at the outside washhouse, and then he appeared, grabbing me for a hug. 'How's my girl?'

'Good.' I told him about the ewe, the lamb and the belt.

He laughed. 'What would you have done if you hadn't had a belt?'

'I don't know.'

'Farmers have to be resourceful. You could have used your T-shirt, your trousers …'

'Not in a paddock so close to the road, I couldn't!'

'Do as I do, and keep some binder twine in your pockets.'

I wondered how long it would take Lester to realise that I did not want him to treat me like an apprentice. Another whole year?

'How have you got on?'

'The sheep ran pretty well. And I had a windfall. Just as I turned into the block I could see something glinting on the ground, and it turned out to be a shifting spanner. Goodness knows how it got there.'

'On our block?'

'Yes. Just into the driveway. If it had been out by the road I would have left it. But finders and keepers is nine-tenths of the law.'

Oh, no. Not again. Here came those husband-induced giggles. I tried to laugh silently, but Lester saw me clutching the island for support as he turned from filling a glass at the fridge.

'Are you laughing at me again? I'll teach you a lesson.' He grabbed and tickled me until I was rolling on the floor begging him to stop.

'Pull me up and I'll tell you something nice.'

'What?'

'Pull me up.' He did.

'You know you've been wanting me to tell you when I felt ready to have a baby?'

'Yes.' His eyes lit up and his grin widened.

'I'm ready.'

We knew that, for us, starting a family was not going to be as simple as the mere decision to do so. Until recently my life had been very different, and I would never have believed myself to be a woman to whom motherhood would become at all important. Before meeting Lester I had made a decision that I would try not to have children. This was partly because of the various men with whom I had been involved. There always seemed to be a worrying self-centeredness in modern relationships. Who'd want to bring a child into the world with someone who always put themselves first?

But I had also felt that my life had been brim-full already, and that there was so much left to do. How could I have time to experience motherhood? So the years had gone on, I had lived out most of my dreams, and said goodbye to the other men.

Now and again people asked me, as people will, 'Do you have children?' Always my mental reaction was: how could I? – I'm too young – life is only just beginning for *me*.

Four years before my marriage, at age thirty, I had violent and prolonged stomach pains, investigative surgery, and an emergency operation. An adhesion was obstructing my bowel. It appeared that I was prone to adhesions, since X-rays also revealed that my ovaries were adhered to my uterus, although they functioned normally. Later tests showed that in a related problem, the fallopian tubes were blocked and that I would be unlikely to conceive naturally.

At first this had not bothered me unduly, but shortly afterwards I had met Lester. He was ten years older than me and until then had largely sacrificed personal life to the establishment of a successful farm business. I recognised in him goodness, trustworthiness, and a deep love of children. Realising very early in the relationship that it could develop into a long-lasting one, I felt it only right to tell him of my fertility problem. His reaction was swift and strong. He told me that he respected my honesty and that he would help me to overcome the problem, should we stay together. And if the problem could not be overcome, so be it—we would be with each other.

In the security of the bond that was developing between us, my desire for a child had been able to grow. Lester had asked me to tell him when I felt ready to tackle the problems that we were going to have to face if we were to have a family.

Chapter Two

Following an operation to clear my blocked fallopian tubes, we spent twelve months trying to conceive naturally – twelve months that had taken me to age thirty-six and to an increased sense of urgency. I asked my doctor about the next step, and he ordered a hysterosalpingogram. It sounded straightforward enough, when he explained that it was an X-ray of the uterus, ovaries and tubes to see if they had blocked again. I'd had X-rays before, and they had never been painful.

But this one would be. A catheter would be passed through my cervix to the fallopian tubes to inject dye into them. If the dye passed through, there was no blockage. Not until I was undressing for the test did I first understand what was to be done, and promptly asked whether Lester could come into the X-ray room with me.

'Of course,' the nurse replied. It was funny seeing him dressed in a bulky leadened coat that would protect him from the radiation. I squeezed his hand tightly as the discomfort grew. But I have always had an objective interest in medicine, and it was fascinating, that first sight of myself from the inside on the X-ray monitor. The dye was released, and then there was a short wait.

'What can you tell us?'

'Well,' the radiographer had replied, 'your gynaecologist will get the results of this and explain it to you.'

'Can't you tell us anything?'

'The test isn't absolutely conclusive, of course, but it appears as though your tubes have scarred and blocked again.'

'Enough that I wouldn't be able to get pregnant?'

'I think so.'

I cried with frustration that the year, from this point of view, had been wasted. Later, as we dealt with the account at the desk, thoughts of other possible options came to me. 'Do you know anything about IVF?' I asked the nurse, who replied that she didn't know a great deal, as it was a specialised field, but that it would certainly be something worth discussing with a doctor.

The gynaecologist said that IVF would be an option for us, and provided us with a patient handbook from the clinic at which he performed some IVF work to help us make up our minds.

We were astounded at the complexity of the treatment. The picture we had in our minds – a simple one-off procedure joining egg and sperm – was shattered. Replacing it was a jumbled collage of tests, drugs, hormones and operations.

Yet the very complexity of the procedure gave the impression of a guarantee. Every eventuality seemed to be covered, so how could we fail? It was a relatively quick decision to go ahead with treatment. I was concerned at the idea of taking hormones in large doses, but my confidence in the treatment swayed me. I would not be taking them for long.

We were required, first of all, to attend the clinic for tests. Our blood was screened for HIV and hepatitis, and we would not be accepted as IVF patients should either of us suffer from one of these conditions. My hormone levels began to be monitored (which would continue for a month), and Lester had to produce a sperm sample, at an entirely different lab. We attended an information evening, during which we were addressed by one of the doctors from the clinic, one of the lab technicians, a committee member from an infertility support group, and a counsellor employed by the clinic. The counsellor talked at length about When To Stop. We won't have to worry about that, I thought. We'll stop at two!

We were told that the government would cover the bulk of the cost of six cycles. Out of these we might obtain enough embryos to freeze for additional cycles.

The statistics seemed promising: about twenty-five per cent of couples would succeed on their first cycle, twenty-five per cent of those remaining would succeed on a second cycle, and so on. I remember looking around the room at all the other couples, wondering.

We were three years into marriage now. I wanted a tangible product of my union with Lester, a being that was partly myself and partly him. I wanted to watch each minute stage of development of a human being, and to teach it to respond to all that Lester and I did about the world. And I wanted to experience pregnancy and birth.

If it was not to be, I could live with that—life would still be full to the brim, just different. But I wanted to know how it was going to be, so as to start living accordingly. I needed the matter settled.

Chapter Three

It was becoming evident that involvement with IVF would mean much time spent away from the farm. Five hours' drive to the city, medical appointments, five hours' return: it would always necessitate staying away at least overnight, and therefore enlisting the help of neighbours, if only to tie up our dogs and pen our poultry. Locals would think that we had nothing on our minds but getting away. So be it.

So far, treatment had taken us away once, for a combination of the blood screens, information evening, and Lester's test. A month had passed since then and now the monitoring of my hormonal pattern was complete, too. All normal, all clear! someone rang to tell us. Apart from my blocked fallopian tubes there should be no reason why I could not bear a child, as everything in my reproductive system was the 'standard model'. I tried to take this as a compliment. So did Lester when it was revealed that his sperm were 'above average'. We were most unsure whether to feel proud of these achievements, which were beyond our control and which would never have been revealed under normal circumstances.

We made an appointment for something called a 'nurse interview': another drive to town, another overnight stay. Unlike city women, who had the option of calling into the clinic each day to be given their injections, or could take the drugs home to inject themselves, I had no choice: I was going to need home injections. At least, I knew from reading the information booklet, I could choose to ask my husband to give me the needles if I preferred. I did prefer! It might take me half an hour to get around to inflicting pain on myself. Lester was not squeamish about giving the needles, and was in fact keen to be involved. But we needed some time with a nurse, to learn what to do.

The word 'interview' connoted another test to pass, but the hour and a half proved more like a training session. The clinic was quiet and empty late on the designated morning, and we were shown straight into an office. In came a bonny, plump, smiling young woman. 'Hi, I'm Annette, and you must be Julia'–shaking hands–'and Lester. I have to take your photos first, for the front of your folder. Stand up!' She gave the immediate impression that everything that we were there to do was going to be easy, fun and worthwhile.

Until, that is, she deluged her desktop with drugs. There were boxes, vials, plastic packets of needles and cotton-wool swabs everywhere.

There were two different drugs. Annette explained their effects and side effects. Lucrin would shut down my hormone system in a sort of 'mini-menopause', termed 'down-regulation'. I was to have a daily injection of it for ten days, then have a blood test taken near home and couriered to Annette. If it showed that my hormone levels were suitably low then, as well as continuing on Lucrin, I would start on a daily dose of the second drug, human menopausal gonadotrophin.

Annette was very jocular. 'Several middle-aged Portugese nuns have been busy producing urine for this drug,' she announced. I made some feeble reply. She went on to explain that HMG would kick-start my ovaries into developing several eggs at once. The clinic insisted on aiming for multiple rather than single egg collection, to maximise chances of producing as many embryos as possible.

Annette explained when I should have blood samples taken at the local hospital and sent by courier to the IVF clinic in the city. There was an optimum time for egg collection and subsequent embryo transfer, revealed by the hormone levels in the blood. She recorded on a chart everything that we had to do. There was so much to remember! Injections every day, tests, phone calls.

As the follicles containing the eggs grew I would be required to come to the city for scans to gauge their size and to work out the best time for egg collection. This was a short operation under light anaesthetic in which eggs would be taken by means of a fine needle. They would then be fertilised with Lester's sperm, grown for two days, and two of them re-inserted as embryos. The extra demands on my system from the drugs, tests and operations would inevitably leave me physically and mentally drained, with swelling, tiredness, nausea and constipation to be expected.

For now, Lester had to learn to prepare, measure and administer my daily injections. Each HMG vial contained a minimal dose of drug powder, but I had been prescribed a larger dose: three vials to be mixed with one of solution, drawn up and bubbled from one vial into the next to collect the three measures of powder. In Annette's office Lester 'practised' by injecting me with pure water. The situation was quite amusing, as his rough farmer's mitts struggled to work gently with the tiny glass bottles and individually packaged syringes. The very serious look on his face betrayed his nervousness at this new experience and his anxiety not to make any mistakes.

Annette was kind enough to notice this. 'You've done really well, Lester,' she said, and he sat back and smiled. 'Julia shouldn't have any worries. But ring at any time if you're unsure of dosages or dates.'

'Will do,' he said.

Annette had gone out of her way to minimise the amount of time that Lester and I would be required to be away from home by helping us to organise blood tests near the farm rather than in the city. As well, she had ensured that we were supplied with the form of HMG that could be injected subcutaneously, like the Lucrin, rather than intra-muscularly, to simplify the number of methods that needed to be learned.

'I wouldn't be surprised if she's from the country herself,' I remarked to Lester as we drove home the next day. 'She seems to take a personal interest in us and the fact that we're on a farm.'

'She did seem very down-to-earth.' But he didn't want to talk. The minute that we left the city behind his mind turned to prioritising jobs awaiting us, and to how fast we could reach home so that he could drive around and check stock.

We were so nervous about using the drugs. We both woke each morning with one thought: to promptly and correctly carry out the injections. This we did religiously at the same time each morning. Two sorts of needles had to be used: one to draw up and mix the solution to the required strength, and one to administer it. The HMG injections were painful, not because of the needle size, but because of the amount of solution being forced under the skin. Lester was very stoic and practical about injecting his wife, and continued depressing the plunger even as I bit my lip and stamped the floor. After all, he had to inject several thousand sheep each year, and they didn't carry on in such a fashion. But he showed more sympathy in taking over the bulk of the farm work, including my usual responsibilities, as my discomfort grew.

Daily we ticked off the injections on the record sheet provided. We dutifully presented for my blood tests, sent them to the city and rang the clinic to see if they had arrived and what the resultant instructions were. These calls often necessitated long and frustrating waits by the phone for a call to be returned, as the clinic was always busy. Sometimes they'd ask, 'Can we return your call?' and I'd be in a dilemma. I was supposed to go feeding hay, or working at the shearing-shed, and we had no mobile phone. So I'd have to ask Lester to do my work for me. As the city visit grew closer we crossed off farm jobs, organised help around the farm during our absence, let the food in the fridge run down, packed and rang my parents to update our ETA. We would be staying with them for however long the 'main' city trip— the one which would hopefully include an embryo transfer— proved to be. It couldn't come soon enough for me.

Chapter Four

There seemed to be an unwritten rule, very quickly trans-mitted, against talking to any of the other patients in the IVF clinic waiting room. I had expected, I now realised, to meet a group of women who were willing, if not eager, to compare notes on their treatment so far. But nobody would look at me directly.

I had been amazed on first entering the waiting room early on a weekday morning to see that nearly every seat was taken. I had added my name to a pencilled list that showed dozens of other women had already been through that morning. My expectations fell: were we, then, not amongst a chosen few, privileged to be undergoing this treatment, but rather just one couple amongst many being churned through the clinic?

I could see at a cautious glance that there were many different 'types' there. Some were quite evidently dressed for their working day to come: a nurse, a policewoman. One looked like a typical lawyer: smart sparse dark suit, commodious briefcase. Others wore tracksuit pants or leggings and bulky tops. (What was it Annette had said?

Something about everyone wearing outsize jumpers as the drugs started to take effect and the tummy swelled.) Ages were more homogenous—apart from one or two who looked barely out of school, most were well into their thirties.

Anyway, I thought, I can live with none of them looking particularly friendly. I won't need much emotional support, since we'll only have to go through this once, maybe twice at the most. Some of these women must have real problems. It would be quite awful having to endure treatment time and again, never knowing whether the effort would be worth it. Lester and I would be able to quite enjoy it all as a fascinating experience to tell our child later in life.

Of course, the trip to the city that IVF necessitated would also be a pleasant break away from the farm. And if I did need someone to talk to—well, Lester was there. How many of these other women had their husbands by their side this morning? Two, I counted, out of maybe twenty-five. There are many advantages to farming, I thought. Even if leaving the farm entailed some extra effort and organisation, it was possible to get away together. And I was glad that after this visit to the clinic I faced not a full day's work in an office somewhere, but a few shopping errands, a cappuccino, then a quiet afternoon odd-jobbing for Mum and Dad. My tummy was sore, and my whole system felt out of sync. I decided that next time I felt completely well I would make a conscious effort to appreciate it.

I glanced at my watch. Ten minutes to go until the scan appointment time we'd been allocated. My blood had been taken ten minutes earlier. (In the clinic jargon, which I'd already assimilated, it was never 'blood test' or 'sample', just 'blood'.) Better get used to a lot of waiting around. I took a look at Lester. His arms were folded across his chest as though he didn't know what to do with them on this enforced day of leisure. His feet were placed well apart. I noticed a burr stuck in his sock. His face was turned away from me, looking at the TV screen showing 'Good Morning Australia'. There were going to be husband-calling, billy-tea drinking and uphill cowpat-shovelling competitions today at someplace called Cooee Bay.

'We'll practice up the paddock and enter one year, what do you think?' I whispered. Lester's laugh was quiet; the atmosphere wasn't conducive to talking in a normal tone.

A couple came out of the scan room, crossed the waiting room, and left.

Why does everyone look so non-committal? I kept thinking. Surely we should all be trying to remember every detail so we can later tell our children who result from all this treatment.

My glance fell on the raised shelf at the end of the receptionist's counter. Books and videos were displayed there, with a computer-printed sign that said: 'Enquire here if you would like to borrow any of these.' *Surviving Infertility*. *Why Me? The Empty Cradle*. I felt a pang of pity for the couples who needed such books.

A door opened at the far end of the waiting room. I nudged Lester. 'There's Annette.' We both caught the eye of 'our' nurse (we knew nothing of the others she interviewed) and exchanged smiles with her. She'd given us such special help. Despite it, I thought, it appeared that a minimum of ten days away from home would be necessary. But it would soon go. Coffee and shopping with Fiona tomorrow, dinner with Liz and Matt tonight, a visit to our nieces, several errands to complete around the city, and one or two outings with Mum and Dad would pass the time. Better keep the end of the week relatively quiet, as the clinic advised a rest day around the time of 'egg pickup'.

'Julia.' The door of the scan room was open and an attendant stood there smiling. Lester gathered up the bag and umbrella, remarking: 'We're in early – good-oh.'

The radiologist ushered us into the darkened room. 'Hi Julia, Lester; I'm Robyn – I don't think we've seen you here before.'

'No – it's our first cycle.'

'Okay. No doubt you're keen to see what effect the drugs have had on you. You're from the country, are you?'

'Yes, we're on a farm five hours' drive away.'

'When did you come up?'

'Yesterday.' I am never particularly talkative. I have the introvert's habit of always waiting to gauge a stranger's reaction to anything I say, before expanding.

'We've had quite a few country people lately. In fact I think one of last month's pregnancies was a lady from out your way. There's also a city address listed for you here.' Her finger marked a place in a cardboard file. 'Is that where you're staying?'

'Yes, it's my parents' place. The phone number should be there for instruction calls.'

'Yep. Good. Now, slip your bottom things off and hop up here. Lester, you take a seat there where you'll be able to see the screen too.' We followed instructions while Robyn busied herself adding something to the file. She turned just as I was settling myself.

'Back a bit lower and feet in the stirrups. Just relax and I'll explain the equipment to you. This is an ultrasound scanner, and while this rod may feel a little cold and uncomfortable it shouldn't hurt you. I'm just going to insert it and it will show us both of your ovaries and whether or not your follicles are growing under the stimulating drugs. So here we go. There's your bladder – we've kept you waiting by the look of it!'

My eyes and Lester's met just long enough to acknowledge surprised amusement.

'Now your left ovary is coming into view.' She paused, and there were several clicking noises. 'I'm measuring the follicles. They need to be around sixteen millimetres each to be of any use to us. You have three here that are growing well but they're not quite ready, so you'll probably need to come in for another scan. Now the right ovary. Oh, this is good. There are several here that might develop quite nicely.'

Both halves of the patient team were looking avidly at the screen. I couldn't tell what Lester was thinking as he squeezed my hand, but my own inevitable thought was that I might be looking at one half of our future child.

And yet if Robyn had not been there to explain, it would have been difficult to tell exactly what we were looking at. The contents of the screen looked like a litter of black, white and grey splotched kittens rolling in leisured pleasure. The splotches, I realised, were the key elements, and I focused on their size and bean-like shape to keep my mind from succumbing to ticklish discomfort.

The examination continued for perhaps five minutes, with still shots being taken that would be seen by a doctor later that day and interpreted.

'Do you know what day I'm likely to have the egg pickup? It's just that we'd half arranged to meet some friends on Friday.' I was used to a busy life, with each element slotting into its place.

'I can't say for sure. Maybe Thursday. But we'll have to ring you this afternoon. You do know, don't you, that you'll need to be near the phone every afternoon while you're here in case there's something we need to tell you to do?'

'Yes, okay.'

'Here are some tissues and there's a washbasin in the corner. Good luck if I don't see you again.'

'Thanks.' We're clearly being dismissed, I thought. 'Can you tell us, though, if that's a good number of follicles to have developed – I mean, I've heard of women having twenty or more eggs removed.'

The clinician's look betrayed her – she had been asked that question too many times before. 'Yes, some women do produce that many eggs, but it's not the quantity that's important but the quality. You could have only two or three eggs removed but if they fertilise and grow well you may well be one of those who get pregnant in this month's group.'

'Right. So we're doing quite well then.'

'You're doing fine. Of course, if you end up with some spare embryos and manage to have a frozen cycle later as well, that's very good too. Okay?'

'Yes.'

'Enjoy the rest of your day then.'

Lester and I did not speak as we dodged feet and furniture to get to the lift but once alone we were eager to compare impressions. I was feeling disappointed. 'I know she said we're doing quite well, but I suppose I expected more large follicles because my tummy's grown so much and because we've had to put in so much effort and everything.'

'It's about what I expected. I think we should be quite pleased. At least some have grown – it would have been terrible if the drugs had had no effect at all, wouldn't it?'

'Hm.'

'Come on, chin up my girl. We'll get there. I'm excited – like she said, it's the quality that matters.'

'Okay. I'm feeling really tired all of a sudden.' I couldn't understand why: it was 8:30 in the morning. 'A coffee might help – do you want to go down the road here?'

'Righto.'

As we strolled, choosing amongst the many outdoor cafés, I adopted something of a holiday mood. I had heard tell of the traumas of IVF, but could not see them. Life seemed about as traumatic as an afternoon at the Royal Show.

Chapter Five

It was mid-morning when we returned to my parents' house on the southern side of the city, about half an hour's drive from the clinic. Mum and Dad had only recently moved there, but I felt very much at home and knew that Lester did too. Despite this he sometimes found the suburban conditions—the high-fenced small garden, and the close proximity of neighbours and their noise—unbearably claustrophobic, and had to escape for a few minutes to an adjacent grassy reserve.

Lester and I had decided on a general policy of keeping our IVF treatment a secret from all but a few people, fearing the need for repetitive explanations and having to face the intrusiveness that is often a feature of small communities. But we would have involved my mother and father even were it not for the fact that some practical support was needed for the city visits. A place to stay, a phone number to give to the clinic for the daily instructions to be conveyed, a kitchen in which I felt free to prepare the type of food my body craved while I tried to cope with the side-effects of the fertility drugs—these were all important. Much more so, however, was the opportunity to share with someone else the excitement of what we were going through.

It was exciting – each injection, each blood test was easy to endure because it brought us one step closer to our goal of having a child. In a few days' time our child would be conceived, we would see it on a video screen in its first days after conception and I would soon knowingly be carrying it inside me. These were enlivening thoughts. Every step of the way felt like an achievement deserving of someone's admiration and interest, and parents could provide these quite well.

Particularly, of course, when by definition they were also prospective grandparents, and so had a further stake in the success of the enterprise. They constantly tell us that they only want this child for our happiness, I thought as I saw my parents opening the front door, and that it won't matter one way or the other to them personally. So why are their faces so eager?

I looked forward so much to times when our child would be with them. I wanted that child to inherit the enthusiasm for life that runs in our family. There was Mum, looking twenty years younger than her actual age, elegant and proud precisely because of her determination to pack life to the full. Dad was loving and good, quiet and conscientious, a homebody who'd retired to peace and private pursuits just as soon as he could and who had been living contentedly ever since.

'How did it go?' As usual, no restraint from Mum.

'Are you all right?' A little more concern for his daughter's comfort from Dad.

'Yes, Dad, I'm fine. Nothing hurt at all – in fact we

enjoyed it because it was so new and exciting. Everybody at the clinic – all the patients – are so serious though. Unhappy serious. Anyway, with the scan – I guess I'm a bit disappointed because I expected to see more growth.'

'Haven't the drugs done you any good then?'

'Oh, yes …' The explanation took almost as long as had the actual tests themselves. Although Mum and Dad had borrowed and read the explanatory booklet provided to couples involved in IVF and had professed to understand it, their retention of the contents was not as good as if it was all actually happening to them, rather than around them. It was hard to explain everything, anyway, without becoming gynaecological and seeing embarrassment battle with composure on Dad's face. He probably imagined the whole process as excruciatingly painful and intrusive, rather than just uncomfortable and tiresome as it had been so far. Talking about it was a matter of resorting to euphemisms in Dad's presence, then giving a fuller and more detailed description when alone with Mum, leaving her to share what she would with her bemused but intensely caring husband.

They had grandchildren already – my brother's little girls – and would have loved to see us parents, but put no pressure on us. Theirs was a quietly hopeful 'wait and see' attitude. After hearing about our morning and showing Lester an area of the garden that he could help to reshape, Dad returned to erecting a rainwater tank, Mum to potting a plant.

Being with my parents reminded me that it had been a while since we had spoken to Lester's mother. 'Do you think you ought to ring your mum?' I asked. 'She'll be wanting to hear about our progress.'

'I'll give her a call tonight.'

My mother-in-law's attitude was similar to that of my own parents. Widowed, she lived for most of each year near Lester's sister interstate and enjoyed helping out with her young and large family. As a result we did not see a great deal of her. When we had seen her last we had told her that we had been experiencing trouble in starting a family and that we were going to try IVF. She had accepted the news calmly, warmly wishing us all the best but not imposing her own views in any way.

The first day in the city was thus a quiet one, apart from the tests. The clinic rang in the afternoon to say that 'a blood' would be required the next morning, but no scan. I tried to keep in mind the clinic's system of numbering the days of the stimulant drug cycle: this was Day Nine.

Evening of Day Nine—dinner at Liz's. She was a close friend with whom I had worked many years ago, and when each of us had married an easy friendship of the two couples had developed, too.

Liz and Matthew, city-dwellers, had recently brought their two young sons to the farm. Their visits were frequent and welcome. I knew that for other women, indeed for other couples who were experiencing infertility, spending time with other people's children could be a painful reminder of the lack in their own lives. We had heard tell of childless couples who would go to great lengths to avoid contact with children, foregoing family occasions and letting friendships with child-blessed couples lapse.

But Lester and I had never known these difficulties, and hoped that we never would. We enjoyed having children to stay, whether they were younger members of the family or the children of friends. The heartbeat of the house would quicken for a few days, we listened to childish laughter and chatter, we would relax our normal standards of tidiness. Farm jobs would take twice as long as normal but have a sense of fun about them. We would enjoy a taste of the future, then appreciate the restoration of our peace.

So the presence of James, six, and David, four, was always a pleasure. However, I had not been able to enjoy their most recent visit as much as I normally would. I had felt tired, preoccupied, uninterested in what was going on in everyone else's life. Affected by the IVF drugs, whose strength I had not anticipated, I had wanted to explain to my friend the reason for my uncharacteristic lack of energy and enthusiasm at the time. And so the secret had been shared.

I wonder, I thought now, whether Liz has become any more understanding of what we're doing. For my friend's reaction had surprised me. It was not that she had said anything directly disapproving, but rather that there had been a lack of the enthusiastic support that I had expected to be forthcoming from Liz.

She knew that we very much wanted to become parents, and knew also that we had been trying to do so for some time without success. Liz had always been, if anything, more strongly maternal than me, and I had deliberately shown great interest in her pregnancies and children. She certainly returned this interest – she knew little of what the IVF program involved and took the opportunity to find out as much as she could from me. But while she and Matthew had departed wishing us luck, Liz left me with the distinct impression that she disapproved in some way of the whole process.

'Did you feel it too?' I'd asked Lester after the farm visit was over. He hadn't but he did not know Liz or her moods well.

'You could always ask her what she really thinks.'

'Mm, I know I could, but it's tricky because really what does it matter what she thinks? I mean, it's not going to change our minds and stop us from going ahead, is it? I guess I'm just surprised and a bit afraid that it might affect our friendship—it's the first time I've felt disapproval of any sort from her.'

Further thought had gradually led me to conclude that it was probably Liz's more traditional outlook that was preventing her from accepting the IVF treatment as a good idea. She'd always taken a conventional view of life, whereas I was the rock-the-boat type. I suppose we'd been fascinated by the tug of war between each other's philosophies, and perhaps this was one of those occasions when she carried in her head some principle that had never occurred to me. I knew that some people saw IVF as a form of playing God, playing with life, but although a Christian myself it had never entered my head to question that Lester and I were doing everything in our power to create life, and that there could be nothing wrong with that.

Moreover, I had to remember that this news was going to come as a surprise to people and that I must allow them time to react. Liz was the first person that I had told, apart from my parents, and her reaction was probably going to be typical of many people's.

Now, on Day Nine, Liz's greeting was warm and

welcoming to both of us. She looked fresh, cool, dressed in white pants under a matching tunic, her hair recently cut in her usual bob. She seemed to cope so well with fitting all the demands of her life around motherhood, despite constantly professing inadequacy.

'Tell me how you're feeling now,' she demanded of me, in a way that gave the impression that she really did want to know. 'I'm behind though, as usual,' she added, 'chasing after these two, but you can tell me while I get you to chop some fruit, if you don't mind.'

There was little opportunity to really talk, with the attention of Auntie Julia and Uncle Lester greedily claimed by two lively little boys who had much with which to impress their visitors: sweetcorn growing in a pot, bike-riding skills and an imaginative Lego construction. I was forced to abandon the fruit salad.

'Are you going to chase me with the broom?' James demanded. At the farm he'd run squealing around the garden as I aimed my straw broom at him for such terrible infringements as yelling 'boo!' at the ducks or swinging on the garden gate.

'No, because I haven't got my broom today, but ... I've got hands to tickle you with!' More squeals.

'When I come to the farm again are we going to go crashing through the bushes?' was David's concern. I'd—foolishly, I suppose—let him steer the ute over clumps of bulrushes, all the while keeping my fingers crossed that there were no lambs hiding there.

'Instead of that I think we might stay on the tracks and you can see how straight you can drive. How would that be?'

'Cool.' They were definitely sweetest when they were easily satisfied.

'I've got a footy, Uncle Lester,' James announced.

'Right. We'll take it over the road to the playground and you can show me your technique.'

Half an hour spent in the park saw Matt pull up.

We returned to the house and shared a lively family meal.

It wasn't until the two boys had been protestingly placed into bed, and coffee and Bailey's were being offered, that a coherent adult conversation could be pursued. The talk was of common interests: education, travel, family.

'So how are things looking for you now? How did the morning's tests go?'

Liz's question relieved me of the feeling that this topic was being avoided. 'Pretty well. The drugs have had a good effect, and we look like getting a reasonable number of eggs retrieved.'

'Are they all girl eggs? David deliberately scratched the piano with a twenty-cent piece this morning.'

'Well, take what comes. At least he's alive and healthy.'

'He's certainly that. I guess the second one always seems livelier because suddenly it's double trouble.' She sipped her coffee. 'You might get twins you know, and get the whole family all in one go. How'd that be?'

Matt affected a 'simpleton' voice and interrupted. 'Long as they's strong enough to pull a plough Ma n' Pa'll be happy.'

Lester laughed and said that he liked the idea of the kids eventually working off the cost of the IVF cycle, but I tried to give Liz the answer she was looking for. 'It'd be all right. We'd prefer just one, but it's quite possible that we'll have twins because we're supposed to be having two embryos transferred. Even if we only had one transferred it could split into two, in theory.' We knew, anyway, that the clinic aimed for single births as much as possible, and that there were strict limits on the number of embryos to be transferred.

'Yes, twins could work,' Liz commented. 'One sleeping at home and one riding in the tractor, or whatever. Reminds me, Julia, Tricia at work had twins.'

'No kidding,' I mumbled. I'd just bitten into a crumbly slice.

'Do you mind if I ask you another question?' Liz added.

Lester replied. 'No.'

'Are you sure?'

'Of course,' Lester said. 'We'd hardly have told you about this without expecting that you might ask us something about it from time to time. Fire away.'

'Okay, I will. And I—we're—not being judgmental when we ask this, we're curious.'

'Mm—fine.'

Liz looked at the floor, harder-faced, choosing her words. 'How can you go ahead, knowing that you might create a life and then have to destroy it?'

I was shocked, but tried not to show it.

'Not give it every chance at life, you mean don't you sweetheart?' Matt had prompted.

'Oh, yes.'

'What do you mean?'

'Well, this treatment is stimulating you to produce more eggs than usual, isn't it?'

'Yes.'

'And the idea of that is to increase your chances by creating as many embryos as possible?'

'Right.'

'Well, what if the first one you ever use ... "takes", for want of a better word, and you don't need the others. What happens to them?'

'I see what you're getting at.' Lester and I inquired of each other in a glance: who would do the talking? I would. 'We had to sign a consent form, saying in that event whether we would want our embryos frozen for later use, given to another couple, given to research, or discarded.'

Liz was eager, and butted in. 'And doesn't having to make that decision put you off the whole thing? I mean, how do you decide?'

'I guess for us ... Without telling you what we've actually decided on paper, we don't think it will come to that anyway. The decision wasn't that difficult because I think we both feel that we're probably not going to have many excess anyway, that we may have a few, and that we'll freeze some and give them all a chance at life later. We're never going to just leave any there.'

'No. We're not being judgmental. Just wondered what it's like to have to decide.'

'No, I know. I'm glad you asked. We're coming from different mindsets I suppose. We're not going to deny this chance at life by being really scrupulous about ethics. If we took that to its logical conclusion, I'd have never used contraceptives. The potential of life isn't life itself, is what I suppose I mean.' I paused, waiting to be agreed with. 'I don't think there's anything wrong with this. I mean, people trying to get pregnant in the ordinary way create lots of embryos that never take.'

'True.'

'We're never going to keep on having drug cycles and creating more embryos to store up while we've already got some frozen.'

It was as though the men were elsewhere, while Liz and I struggled to regain a feeling we had always taken for granted: that of seeing the same view along the way, even if we sought different destinations.

'How are you going to feel about ones that don't succeed, though? That they're easily replaced?'

'No! Absolutely not! I'm going to feel that each one is a total individual with unique potential, and I'll grieve over it, I'm sure.'

'We both will,' Lester added. Funnily enough, however, this was the first time that either of us had really stopped to think of what our feelings might be in the event of failure.

'It's really tricky, isn't it?' Matt finally broke in. 'It all depends on when you think a life begins – the moment of conception, or the embryo implanting, or both, or what.'

'Of course.'

While consensus could not be reached, the openness had at least created a space across which feelings could start to move together. I felt that there had been an indefinable shift in Liz's understanding, and it eased my mind.

I don't want people to make me feel, I thought on the drive home, as though motherhood has to come naturally and that I'll only find fulfilment through work and that I'm supposed to just accept that ... oh, these bloody drugs are making me over-emotional.

One other person came in on the secret. Fiona was another dear old friend, although I did not often get the opportunity to see her. She had recently returned from a

long stint overseas and we had arranged to meet near the
IVF clinic to spend the morning together after my Day Ten
blood. There would perhaps be another get-together with
our fellows later in the week, depending on how treatment
was going. But for today's meeting both of us were going to
insist on coming alone. Much as I valued the way my
husband wanted to do everything together, and the fact that
he would always accompany me to the clinic even for a
simple blood test in case it left me feeling less than my best,
there were times when I wanted to be the Julia who
someone else had always known, and this was definitely
the case today. Lester had been with me when we had welcomed Fiona back into the country, but apart from that I
had not seen her since she had flown briefly back from
London to be at my wedding. It was one of those friendships that could be interrupted by geographical distance for
years at a time and resume unaffected.

'You're looking good!' Fiona exclaimed.

'Whatever you do don't say I'm looking 'bonny' as my
mother-in-law sometimes does—it generally means I'm half
a stone overweight! Look at this stomach.' I flapped open
my jacket to show a distinct pot belly. 'That's what the
drugs do to you.' Fiona had already been told about IVF in
a long recent phone call. (I had afterwards said to Lester:
'I won't tell anyone else—I promise! It just sort of all came
out because Fiona would have known something was going
on, anyway.')

We spent the morning coffee-shop-hopping: talking was
easier sitting down than wandering around the streets or the
shops. Fiona wanted to know every detail of IVF and how I
was feeling about it, seeking to share in the experience as

though it were merely a pregnancy with some unusual preliminary matters. To be able to talk in this way was exhilaratingly unrestrictive, and I did not feel ashamed of my confidence in the program.

'I mean, I've got eggs and Lester's got sperm, and all they need to do is to put them together and put them back in me—there's nothing at all wrong with me except blocked tubes, apparently.'

'It should work for you at some stage then.'

'We're really confident it will work soon. And enthusiastic.'

'I can see that.'

I grinned and pressed bits of icing, dropped from a Danish, onto my fingertip. Women of my generation had grown up knowing how easy it was to fall pregnant: we'd been constantly warned about it throughout adolescence. And I was thinking of the information evening Lester and I had attended, that had given me the impression that success rates at the clinic were about the same as those of natural attempts at pregnancy. One in five cycles would succeed, I remembered. Or was I interpreting the statistics the way I wanted to?

Fiona asked another of her many questions about the treatment. 'How do they know when to take the eggs out and put the embryos back in?'

'A blood test every day—it all goes on hormone levels. Anyway, to other things—you and Robert think you may be heading to Sydney, but is there any chance that you'll get down and see us before then?'

'I'm hoping next month sometime … or I might have to come on my own if Robert gets interviews.'

'That's fine. You can always come down together at some later stage.' I was proud of the farm, and eagerly pressed old city friends to visit so that I could show off in my new role.

'Will that coincide with the end of your two weeks' waiting to see if you're pregnant? Would that be a really bad time for me to come, or would I be able to help you through it? You just say, because I don't want to be in the way.'

'It might happen to be at the same time, but that'd be good, I think. I'll need someone to talk to either way, and they say you should have something else to look forward to at the end of the two weeks in case you just get a big disappointment. I'm not the going to pieces type, anyway.'

So plans were made.

Chapter Six

Shortly after midday I stepped onto the bus to return to the suburbs, having thoroughly enjoyed my morning. But feeling so tired—uncharacteristically, overwhelmingly tired. I chastened myself out loud in front of my family for being so 'weak', scoffed at Lester's suggestion that I go and lie down ('In the middle of the day?!'), and aroused an angry reaction in my mother.

'You're supposed to rest! Stop worrying about how much you can get done while you're here and enjoy the chance to do nothing. My weeds will still be there in the morning!'

With so much encouragement to do what I really felt like doing anyway, it was easy to give in and sleep.

Lester later told me of a conversation that he and my parents had at the time.

'She won't learn, will she?' Mum complained to him. She was reading half the newspaper, and he sat down and picked up the other half.

'What do you mean?'

'She always thinks the measure of the value of a day is how much she can get done in it, and she's trying to be no different on these drugs. I'll bet you any money the ones who succeed on this program are the ones who don't have much going on in their lives. Who can take it easy and relax through the whole ordeal. Julia's trying to behave as she would on any of your other trips to us — gadding about all over the place. She's actually got a list of jobs she wants to get done. And I bet you've both been working hard right up until the minute you left, haven't you? So that you've arrived tired, I mean.'

Lester admitted this. 'It was a case of having to keep working to make up for the time we'll be away. We were forced to give up on some jobs that we would normally do, but there are some that have to be done regardless.'

'Now you know I wasn't criticising.'

'You'll grab every chance you can to interfere, I know that.' He winked.

'Cheeky. Are you worried about the work you've left — what is it?'

'It's not stock work. Anything to do with the stock just has to be done, that's why I've been flat out crutching until we got away, so we're pretty organised for shearing by the time we get back. No, the sorts of chores I've left are thistle-spraying, maintenance jobs. There'll just be a few more thistles by the time I do get around to spraying, I suppose. This is far more important.'

'You could have stayed home and got the work done, couldn't you Lester?' Dad joined in. 'I think the fact that you haven't and that you've come to support Julia says a lot.' Dad thought — thinks — very highly of Lester.

'Well, I always work on the idea of priority jobs. Whatever's the priority gets done, and right now this is the priority.'

'And how are you feeling about it all at this stage?' Mum asked.

'Quietly positive.' He did not meet her eyes. He did not want to express to my parents his concern that his wife was having to go through everything that the treatment entailed, or his anxiety over what might go wrong. He was only accepting the risks and difficulties because he felt it would all soon be worthwhile.

After a pause Dad asked: 'Did you want to ring the fellow who's keeping an eye on the farm? Just go ahead if you want to.'

'Thanks. I may do, but I'll wait until we've been here a few days first.'

And so the week went on. Daily blood tests and scans following my two injections and a hasty breakfast. The occasional 'morning off' from tests. Attempts to keep in touch with a friend or family member each day, shopping, taking a share of cooking. Walking our own little dog and Mum and Dad's.

Waiting to be told that the next stage of the process had been reached. It was, five days after the first scan. A third scan, that morning, showed that the follicles had suddenly and considerably enlarged. A phone call came in the afternoon, and involved instructions for a 'scheduling injection': one that completed the maturation of the eggs, and was precisely timed to maximise the success of the egg pick-up operation.

'Julia—it's Jo from the clinic. How are you?'

'Not too bad.'

'You've been allocated for egg pick-up Thursday morning at 9:15, so that means you need your scheduling injection at 9:15 precisely tonight. You're coming in to the hospital for that, is that correct, rather than doing it yourselves?'

'Yes.'

'And you've filled in your admission form for day surgery?'

'Yes.'

'Now you'll need to get to the hospital on Thursday morning by about seven, and we'll need Lester's contribution here at the clinic at around the same time. Anything else you need to know?'

'Yes. Can Lester come into surgery?'

'No, afraid not. Apparently there have been some problems in the past with husbands getting upset when they thought their wives weren't properly anaesthetised, not realising it's only supposed to be a light anaesthetic. One fellow even punched the surgeon out cold!'

'You're kidding!'

'No—we know Lester's not like that, but all the same we have to abide by the rules.'

'I suppose.' But I was disappointed, because we both wanted to be fully involved in all stages of the process.

'Good luck. You know you needn't come in in the morning—you have a day off, and no injections.'

'Yes.'

'We'll see you Thursday.'

'Bye.' I hung up. 'It's Thursday, everybody …'

I felt almost as excited as if I were to be actually giving birth, or having a Caesarean, on Thursday. Something definite was going to happen, and a time had been allocated to it. And meanwhile, a pleasant rest day tomorrow that seemed like recompense for all the obedient trips into town to have scans and bloods done. Just one more injection, tonight. It was a nuisance having to go all the way into town just for that, but back in our first nurse interview I'd seen the length and thickness of the needle to be given to me intramuscularly, and Annette had asked if we felt competent to do the scheduling injection ourselves. No—I wanted a professional to administer it. Lester had only given me subcutaneous injections so far, and I didn't want him practising another technique with such a tool in his hand.

'Well, what shall we do tomorrow?' I enquired of the rest of the family.

'Don't you be so eager to be filling the days up—you're supposed to take it easy.'

'Oh, Mum, that's after the egg pick-up.'

'But you've been complaining every day of feeling exhausted and needing to sleep all the time—why not thank your lucky stars that tomorrow you don't have to go anywhere, and just relax with a book or your cross-stitch, or maybe take the dogs for a quiet walk?'

'Because we're only here every few months, and there's plenty of time to read and walk and cross-stitch at home. Let's go to that Open Garden we saw advertised.'

'I think your mother's right—you should be taking it easy.'

'Whose side are you on?' I pretended to glare at my husband.

'So what time's this injection tonight?' Mum asked.

'Nine-fifteen. We'd better leave here at half-eight. Dad, could you please tape 'Mad About You' for me?'

'Yes,' (very patiently), 'mark it in the book for me.'

The military precision involved in the scheduling injection amused us. When we arrived at the hospital that night nurses were waiting for us and we were recognised, but we were not allowed in a minute too soon or too late. We both found it hard to believe that the injection could be expected to have its effect just when I was due to go into theatre, but that was the implication. I also had to laugh wryly at how painless the injection turned out to be.

'You could easily have given it to me!' I said. 'We've come into town for nothing.'

'Oh, well. We'll know next time.'

'Yes, but let's hope we don't even need a next time.'

'No, that's right. How are you feeling – tired?'

'Mm. What a blissful thought – sleep-in in the morning. No 5.30 alarm to get us to the clinic.'

'I thought I might get you up to wash the car, now you're in the habit of an early rise!'

'Just try waking me!'

Nobody did try waking me until after ten the next morning. When he brought me a cup of tea in bed Lester told me that Mum and Dad were already preparing their mid-morning coffee.

'There isn't much of the day left for an outing!' I reacted.

'What outing?'

'We're going to the Open Garden.'

He was silent.

'What?' I pressed.

'We're here to bloody well try and get pregnant, not go gallivanting around the country.'

I was shocked that he could be unpleasant while we were

on holiday, and even more determined to have my walk in the hills. Part of me was rebelling against the sudden phenomenon of the rest of the world knowing what was best for me, and trying to plan all my time. 'I want some exercise, and it's not hot.'

No reply. The onus was on me to make small talk to gauge the state of his mood from his reactions.

'I wonder how the stock are at home.'

'I'll ring tonight.'

'What's the matter?'

'I just wish you'd rest while you can. Why do we need so much activity every day? You should be sitting still.'

'I can't sit still and do nothing. When have you ever known me do that? I don't know how.'

At last he looked at me, but he was scowling. 'Well, you're not to walk far.'

'Whatever.'

The garden we visited was glorious—well-designed, full of novel features, laden with colour, but my walk was spoilt. I was too conscious of Lester being aware how awfully tired I felt. It was as though on the granted rest day, with a reprieve from the need to keep going, my body had given into fatigue. My eyes smarted and pulsed, and I wanted to grind my fists into them. My forehead was hot and my limbs ached. And I was cross that everyone else was right.

I would be extremely glad when tomorrow came and the result of the drug-taking was known. It's weird, I thought, but it's almost as if the object of all this is the number of eggs retrieved, not an actual pregnancy. It would be easy to fall into the trap of thinking that you were going along well on

IVF simply because your egg-retrieval rate was good, when you had no chance of ever getting pregnant for some reason or another.

That night over dinner Dad raised yet another 'good luck' glass to us. If luck was involved in pregnancy, we were in with a good chance. My pretty cut-crystal glass contained water and lemon juice, my usual glass of wine foregone.

'Now remember,' Mum was saying, 'if you don't get a good result tomorrow it's not the end of the world. Just try …'

'… again. Yes, we know.'

Chapter Seven

We both woke before the alarm went off, as you do when it's a travel departure day. The previous evening I had found suitable clothes – a sloppy tracksuit, unfortunately, and no make-up allowed, but at least I could wash my hair and put it up. Important occasions are always more successful when they are also good hair days.

When it was time to produce sperm to fertilise the eggs collected, most men used a room opening off the IVF clinic waiting room while their wives were in day surgery. But the clinic allowed the sperm collection to be done at home. Lester and I took a little time over this together. The creation of our child was to involve some physical love.

It was then a matter of transporting the sperm jar to the clinic as quickly as possible. As we travelled I couldn't resist teasing Lester about 'Baby on Board' signs, car fridges and the like. But I really felt for him as he handed the plain brown paper bag over the counter at the clinic. He was embarrassed doing even that much – what would he have been like if he'd had to 'perform' in the side room and emerge into a roomful of strangers? We made the right decision, I thought.

It was a short walk from the clinic to the day surgery suite where my egg retrieval operation was to be performed. After filling in admission forms, I was asked to wait. Incredibly, there were still two hours to go until the time actually scheduled for my operation—I couldn't understand why we had to arrive so early. In the waiting room were three women of about my age who were already capped and gowned in fetching blue, with matching paper slippers and terry-towelling dressing gowns. There were also two men.

I recognised one of the women: our blood tests had coincided on several mornings during the week, and so our cycles must be matching exactly. I wondered which one of us would get pregnant, or whether both of us would. I knew that I had been recognised but the other woman gave me no acknowledgment. Oh well, I thought, perhaps she's been here a few times before and it is all getting pretty discouraging. Lester and I sat on a long couch and I picked up a magazine. Lester turned slightly to face a TV screen which, this time, was showing 'Play School'.

'Go and have a coffee if you like,' I said to him. 'There's no need for us both to be bored and hungry.'

'No. I'll wait with you.'

'Okay.'

Shortly afterwards another patient appeared from a side room, accompanied by a later-than-middle-aged man. Then I was called, and Lester followed me and the nurse into an office where we were asked to sit down.

'I'm just going to ask you a few questions and do some

checks, then you can meet the anaesthetist and we'll get you prepped.'

'Okay. This is my husband, Lester.'

'Hi. Julia—do you have any allergies?'

'No.'

'Heart problems?'

'No.'

The list went on and on. My blood pressure and temperature were taken and I was weighed. Ugh! I'd gained almost a stone since last weighing myself.

'I didn't know the drugs would have that much effect!'

The nurse laughed slightly. 'Don't forget a lot of that will be just retained fluid. You'll soon lose it again—unless of course you get pregnant, which is what you want, I suppose, isn't it?'

'It is, yes! Do you know who's doing the egg retrieval today?'

'Dr Wallis,' the nurse replied. This wasn't my own specialist, but I tried not to feel disappointed: no doubt the doctors were all competent. 'I'll take you in to see Dr McArthur now, he's the anaesthetist.'

It was the man who had been talking to one of the other women earlier. Must be a regular assembly line of operations for them, I thought as we sat down again: I'm not so sure it's a good thing to be last in line this morning. The doctor ran his eye over the list of questions and answers that the nurse had filled out.

'You've had trouble with anaesthetic in the past, I see. What sort of trouble?'

'It seems to leave me really weakened for days afterwards.'

'You'll be glad to hear that this anaesthesia shouldn't

have too bad an effect on you, as it's really only a light sedative.'

'Actually, I was wondering if I could be awake for the operation and just have enough anaesthetic to take the pain away.'

'Oh – why's that?'

'It's all so interesting and I'd be really fascinated to be aware of what's going on.'

'This is the first time you've had an oocyte retrieval, is it?'

'Yes.'

'We can start off with a light dose and see what your needs are after that.'

Back in the waiting room, after having undergone capping, gowning and the amused scrutiny of my husband, I quite suddenly began to experience strong stomach cramps. I told Lester about it, adding: 'It must be the scheduling injection working. It's getting stronger and stronger.'

'Now we know why they were so fussy about the time of the injection. Whatever it's supposed to do, it had to happen before you go into surgery in three quarters of an hour.'

'Are you in for an egg retrieval?' This came from the woman who had been in to see the anaesthetist just before I had, and who was now sitting to my left. I could hardly believe that a fellow patient had struck up a conversation with me.

'Yes. It's my first cycle. What about yourself?'

'No – I'm in for some more exploratory surgery to see why IVF hasn't worked for us yet. I've had four drug cycles so far.'

'Oh – goodness.' (Oops, I thought. Mustn't sound as though I feel sorry for her, or that she might be wasting her time.) 'Have you needed time off work for this?'

'Yes, it was pretty incredible, but one time I was in the clinic and I bumped into a girl who works in the same bank as I do. Neither of us knew the other was on IVF. We still keep it quiet from other people at work but we're able to cover for one another when we have to be away. I actually have to take more than one day off at a time to get down here – we live a fair way away.'

'Oh, no kidding – we're from the country.'

We went on comparing notes until the other woman was called away, warmly wishing us the best of luck, of course, as she left.

'That felt so great – actually to talk to someone else who's going through it, instead of being all secretive. Why don't people talk more?'

'I don't know. Maybe they get to a stage where they just want to get all the treatment over and done with, and not dwell on it. But I could see you enjoyed talking to her.'

'It's different talking to someone who knows what it's like.'

'How's your tummy now?'

'Awful. But it could still do with a pot of tea and a pile of toast. This fasting business is not funny.'

'Never mind. If I know you, you'll make up for it.'

'Of course.'

The wait became boring, the enforced delay frustrating. Eventually a nurse appeared. 'Lucky last – Mrs Masters.'

'Oh, good.'

'You'll be able to take her home, will you?' This was to Lester.

'Yes. Good luck, darling.' We hugged hurriedly, feeling that we were expected to keep moving.

'Thanks. Enjoy your morning tea.'

'Where's he off to?' the nurse asked as we made our way along a glaringly bright corridor.

'Coffee shop along the street.'

'Lucky bloke. While you're out to it!' She had to make conversation about something.

The theatre shimmered in its newness. It seemed a pity to use it. Nurses fussed and joked around me in an attempt to put me at ease, but I didn't find the situation frightening anyway. Indeed, it was intriguing. I looked for the video screen on which I would be able to watch my own eggs being removed, my own potential children.

Dr McArthur asked me to lie down, then administered anaesthetic. I began almost immediately to feel relaxed and light-headed.

'Hello—I'm Dr Wallis.' His face appeared upside-down above my head, and I tried to smile graciously at him. 'I'll be performing your egg retrieval today. When it's over I'll write on the back of your hand how many we managed to get, so that when you wake up you'll be able to look and know straightaway.'

'Okay—thanks.' I relaxed and closed my eyes. Did a minute go by? Ten? I was probably drifting in and out of a sort of sleep, no longer really interested in proceedings. But some sensations could break through the torpor. *'Ouch!'* I had felt an alarming, cutting pain low down. Immediately there were figures at my side injecting more anaesthetic into the needle in my hand. So much for witnessing my own operation.

I woke, befuddled, to sounds of busy-ness in the recovery room, having seemingly slept for no more than a second but having lost two hours. Disappointment at having missed the whole procedure did not come straight away, as a more urgent thought claimed me.

Hand – hand! I looked at my palm, and there was nothing there.

No babies.

It was amazing how strong a feeling of distress could be even within the post-anaesthetic haze.

'No, sweetie,' (I sensed a nurse at my side) 'look at the back of your hand. There you are – ten. That's good.'

'Mm – thanks.' That is quite good, I thought, relieved to see any number at all. About what we expected from the scans. I allowed my mind to nestle back into relaxation and half-slept for some time, then opened my eyes and spoke to a nurse nearby. 'Is my husband here, please?'

'Hang on, I'll go and look for you. Do you feel ready to sit in an armchair and have him come and sit by you?'

'Yes.'

'Do you know you had quite a bit of bleeding in theatre, which is unusual?'

'No – I felt some pain and they put me right out, which I hadn't wanted, but …'

'It's nothing to worry about. You might just feel a little weaker when you sit up, so go quietly.'

The nurse returned soon. 'Come on then, we'll get you over to a comfy chair.'

Several large recliner chairs were arranged in a semi-circle beyond the nurses' station. Two of the women that I had seen earlier were there, including the woman who had been friendly, and who was now with her husband.

'How did you get on?' she asked me.

'Ten.'

'Good!'

'Yes – not bad.'

Lester was waiting next to an armchair, and he helped me to lower myself.

'How are you feeling?'

'A bit groggy but okay. I haven't got any pain anyway. We got ten eggs.'

'Hey – that's good! Ten possible babies.'

'Mm. But I felt a cut and they put me right out, and the nurse just told me I bled a lot.'

'Oh – you're okay now?'

'Yes, but …' I hadn't realised until now how afraid I was of problems arising that might mean cancelling the cycle – perhaps everything had been going too well so far.

'We'll ask about it. So you didn't get to see anything?'

'No.'

'Never mind.'

A nurse came by. She took my blood pressure, then told me that I could expect some lunch soon, and a visit from one of the IVF clinic nurses. I ate sandwiches and fruit salad, gradually the other morning surgery patients left, and a nurse known to us, Chris, arrived.

'How are you doing, Julia?'

'Not too bad.'

'I see you've had ten oocytes removed. That's good.'

'Yes, about what we thought we'd get.' Our ten eggs were to everyone's satisfaction.

'Now, I've got a sheet here detailing what you need to do for the next few days, or couple of weeks actually. We don't give you this at the same time as your earlier instructions, leading up to egg pick-up, because it would all just be too much to take in all at once. But the down-side is that you have to hear it all straight after your operation. Do you feel up to listening now?'

'Yes.' It was a case of having to be but Lester could take in what I might miss.

'The first thing is that you have a day off tomorrow, and spend it very quietly. Later in the morning you can ring up and find out how many of your eggs fertilised, and then in the afternoon you can ring to find out a day and time for your embryo transfer. You're having two embryos trans-ferred I take it?'

'Yes, but apparently I bled a lot in theatre. Will that affect the success of the transfer – I mean, would that have been bleeding from the endometrium?' I was worried about the lining of the uterus, which should provide a thick 'bed' for the implanting embryo.

'It shouldn't have been. More likely to be just bleeding from the needle piercing the vaginal wall. Don't worry – we wouldn't do a transfer if there was some reason not to.'

'Okay.' But I was struck, for probably the first time, by the extent to which we were trusting every one of the many individuals with whom we were dealing to be as attentive as possible to our case and any problems with it. I would really have liked the bleeding to be checked out further, but it was our first cycle – I assumed that everyone else knew more about my body than I did, and that I shouldn't make trouble.

'Now, say your transfer is Saturday, which it's quite likely to be – two days from egg pick-up. That day you'll be given an HCG injection to support this phase, and you'll need another one on Monday.'

'What's HCG?'

'Human chorionic gonadotrophin. It's the hormone produced by the embedding embryo—it sort of tells your body that you're pregnant.'

'I see.' I didn't really see why my body should be told that it was pregnant, when it wasn't, necessarily, but I was later to come to understand that this hormone could prevent an early period, and that this might just help a 'borderline' embryo to implant.

'When are you going back to your farm?'

'We were thinking of Monday, but we could come through town via the clinic for the injection and then go on home from here.'

'That'd be good. We'll also send you home with another HCG injection and a blood bottle, both to be used on the … eighth, it'll work out to. The blood is just for us to check that your hormone levels are going along okay. If you don't hear from us after that test, then there's no problem. Is this all getting to be too much to take in?'

'No—that's all right.'

'If you don't get a period by the sixteenth, you need to have another blood test and get it to us, to see whether or not you're pregnant.'

'We could just get the blood analysed for pregnancy at a lab near home, couldn't we, rather than send it to you?'

'You could, but the results aren't likely to be as accurate. Here we can take account of drugs that may be showing up in your blood, and a normal test can't. Why—is there a problem with sending a blood here?'

Lester chipped in. 'One of Julia's bloods got lost, after we sent it from a doctor's clinic near home.'

'Got lost?'

'Yes—we established that it got to the city, but it never reached the clinic here. And this blood test—the pregnancy one—would be so crucial that we wouldn't want it to get lost and for there to be a delay.'

If she says, You could always just have another one taken, I'll scream, I thought, but said aloud, 'We might be able to pop back up to town for an overnight trip for that test, if it comes to that.'

Lester agreed, and Chris tried to be helpful: 'It doesn't have to be on that exact day. Wait a couple more days, to be extra sure, and then come up—you might avoid a wasted trip that way. It would be awful to get all the way up here and then get your period.'

'Wouldn't it? We'll think about it, anyway. So, ring up tomorrow morning is the next step?'

'Yes. And good luck!'

'Thanks a lot. See you.'

The bombardment of instructions, new burdens and requirements had all been too much, and I dozed most of the way home. After a welcome (and some concerned questions) from my parents I slept again through the afternoon, while Lester helped Dad fit new shelves to his carport walls. The fact that Lester would not be bored helped me to sleep longer and deeper. Both he and my father were fastidious in the way they approached any task, and I knew that they would work harmoniously.

That afternoon, pressure behind him, Lester rang the farm neighbour who was being paid a small amount to check and feed our stock and to ensure that the windmills were filling the water tanks. Everything was fine.

Chapter Eight

I had hoped to go out the next day, but had to admit that all I really felt like doing was sitting and reading. Besides, there were the two all-important phone calls to make. I knew that I should leave the first until at least ten o'clock, when the clinic nurses would have the morning rounds of bloods, scans and blood analyses out of the way.

At 10:01 I rang, Lester by my side.

'Yes, Julia. It turns out that of the ten eggs you had removed, seven have fertilised, which is pretty good.'

'Seven.'

'Yes, so that means that you're likely to get at least one frozen cycle out of this cycle, if you need it. Ring again this afternoon for the time of your transfer.'

'Okay. Thanks.'

Lester had heard my repetition of the magic number. We hugged each other.

'Seven babies! We've got seven babies in the world right at this very moment! I wonder what they're all like.'

'Congratulations, darling.'

'Yes—congratulations to you, too. I wonder what happened to the other three?'

'Just didn't fertilise, I suppose. If you read the information book they say that only about sixty per cent do fertilise, so we've done well. My above-average sperm, of course!'

'Must be.' I kept sarcasm out of my voice. 'Let's tell Mum and Dad.' They were gardening together, Mum giving directions while Dad dug a hole for a new plant. They stopped to hear the news, reacted with pleasure, and quietly returned to what they were doing. So did Lester, but I couldn't settle. I sat on the arm of the chair where he was reading his farmer's bible: the *Stock Journal*.

'I hope the clinic are looking after our babies—I've got an urge to go and get them all now and bring them home.'

'Have you?'

'I can't believe there are seven little beings out there now—inevitable, unalterable individuals!'

'Yes, it's fantastic.'

'It's like we have children already. This is something that people who get pregnant the ordinary way never know.' I paused and looked around at the walls as if they might provide words to convey the intensity of my feeling. 'Every day of the IVF from now on will be so special, because we'll know there are these children. Are you excited?'

'I am, and I feel very positive.' He smiled at me.

'Me too. Well, hoping, anyway, and praying. Say lots of prayers.'

'I will.'

I untangled the tassel on a cushion with one hand, the other slipping behind Lester's head.

'The trouble is, it'll be that much worse if it doesn't work, because already these children have taken on some individual quality for me. You start imagining them, and if we lose them it'll be actually like losing somebody.'

'Well, don't you go thinking about that. Just think positively. Now, were we offering to cook for your mother tonight?'

'Yup. We'll make a special meal, to celebrate and thank them for having us.'

'Do you feel up to going to the shops or do you want me to go?'

'No, I'll go too. I'll just tell them.'

I bought seafood, and made some good stock for a risotto to go with it. I thought about my parents. As much as the welcome they offered was genuine, they were happy alone, and who was to know when the sanctity and privacy of their home would be restored? They had to be aware of my health needs, be subjected to potential embarrassment as a private area of their daughter and son-in-law's life proceeded around them, and show their own interest and concern but balance this with not putting any pressure on us to 'succeed' at IVF. I had repeatedly thanked them for the role they were playing, but never seemed quite able to get my gratitude out of my system.

Cooking also passed the time until a suitable hour to ring the clinic regarding embryo transfer. I was told that this would take place the following day at 11.30 in the morning and, purely by chance, be performed by our own specialist.

'And do you get to choose which embryos you have put in?' my mother asked that night at dinner. No matter where the conversation meandered during the evening meal, it always seemed to return to IVF. The uniqueness of the experience created a willingness to talk in ways that would at other times be unlikely.

'No, I don't think so. They choose the ones to use, and only show us them on the screen. I wish you could see them, too.'

'Oh well,' Dad said quickly. 'We might be seeing them in nine months' time, instead.'

'Are you feeling better now you're off HMG?' Mum asked. 'What's it been, four days free of it?'

'Yes. I'm tired today, but that's from the anaesthetic, I think. It feels good to be off it—my body's coming back to normal, not all bloated and sore. Goodness knows what effect HCG will have, though.'

'No more drugs, apart from that?'

'No. They offer progesterone backup if you need it, but that doesn't seem to apply to me. My oestrogen–progesterone balance was always pretty good.'

'They're not sure how strong your luteal phase is going to be though, are they,' said Lester, 'until after the first cycle.'

'No, of course not.'

'I read in the booklet,' Mum said,' about LH and FSH. Are yours okay?'

Suddenly, I had to giggle.

'What?' Lester said, looking at me. 'I haven't said anything funny. You've been doing most of the talking.'

'No, it's not you,' I said, reaching for my glass. 'It's the way we're all talking—anybody coming in on this conversation would think we are doctors.'

'We've picked up a lot of medical knowledge in a short time,' Mum said, understanding what was amusing me.

'Yes! Even just a month ago we didn't even know what these things meant!'

'I still don't,' Dad muttered.

Mum hadn't heard. 'So if you get pregnant this time the baby—or babies—*ooh!*—would be born in …'

'July.' Lester already had the answer.

'That'd be a really good time farm-wise, actually,' I chipped in as his business partner. 'We'd have our quietest time of the year coming up, when we would normally take holidays. I'd be heavily pregnant around lamb-marking time, though, so we'd have to get someone in to take my place for that. But that's better than being heavily pregnant during shearing or something. I'd have to sit back and watch someone else do the wool-classing. I'll give up lamb-marking but not wool-classing.'

'Will you still take a holiday, with a tiny baby?'

'I don't know, we haven't really thought about it. Generally we say we would always take our family along with us, and not let it stop us doing things. What do you think, love?' I asked Lester.

'I think we'd still go, depending on where, and the baby's health, and whatever else arises. We shouldn't let ourselves get into a laborious groove.'

I cocked my head at him as I tried to ponder his expression but Mum seemed to have missed the gem and continued the conversation.

'You should go. We always took you along as a baby, didn't we, Norman? We always said that having a baby wasn't going to interfere with our enjoyment of life together. People thought we were mad, camping with a tiny baby. But you were as good as gold, and everywhere we went you got lots of admirers.'

'Cheese and fresh fruit okay everyone?' I asked.

'There's a tiny bit of pie left from last night, Lester,' Mum said, 'do you want it?'

'I'm doing all this eating and not a scrap of work. I'll go back looking like I've been in a good paddock.'

'Well, you have!'

My feelings that evening, and the following morning, surprised me in their intensity. Although the morning would not bring an actual pregnancy, simply the placing of two of my fertilised eggs into my uterus, I felt as excited as if a great gift were being given to me, or I was embarking on a special new phase in my life. It was the fact that we were going to be able to view the embryos beforehand on a video screen that so thrilled me. I imagined one day saying to a child, 'I saw you when you were only a cluster of tiny cells.' I anticipated the two weeks to come, during which I would know that the embryos were inside me and would be able to imagine them and visualise their possible development. Everyday life seemed as though it would shine with newness and purpose.

Chapter Nine

The morning deserved a sense of occasion, and coffee and gooey cakes at an outdoor café helped provide this. At the clinic a familiar nurse greeted us and showed us into an unfamiliar room. It had a huge framed Monet print, a stack of magazines and a bed with stirrups.

'I hate to tell you this, but Dr Connell has been delayed at the other branch and is running half an hour late. Do you mind waiting here, or do you want to go away and come back?'

We were both disappointed, but Lester replied to the nurse: 'We'll stay here, that's okay.'

'There are magazines on the shelf, and I can fetch you a coffee if you like.'

'No, thanks, we've just had one.'

She left.

'What a bummer!'

'Never mind, worse things could happen. Do you want to read?'

I picked up a magazine but just as quickly threw it down again. 'I'm too excited!' I spent the ensuing half-hour looking out of the window or exchanging the occasional word with Lester.

We heard movement and voices in the corridor, but the movement continued into the room next door to ours. The voices emanating from that direction over the next ten minutes made it plain that another couple were undergoing their embryo transfer there.

'I hope they won't be able to hear us,' I said.

'By the time the doctor gets to us this other couple may have left.'

In all it was three-quarters of an hour after the scheduled transfer time before we were attended to. By this time the sense of occasion seemed to have diminished a little.

Eventually a young woman knocked and entered, introduced herself, and explained that she was a lab technician. She proceeded to occupy herself fiddling inside the humidi-crib that she had pulled into the room behind her. She was looking down a microscope, and explained that she was trying to gather our embryos up onto a glass plate over which she could position the camera that would be used to display them. The sense of occasion was re-established.

'You had seven eggs fertilised – unfortunately one embryo fragmented, but four have been suitable for freezing.'

'Four. That's good,' was our consensus.

'Yes. We've frozen them as two, one and one. That way if you need a frozen cycle, and one of the two together doesn't thaw properly, we can thaw another without using all of them.'

'I see. And do you know how big they were?' Lester asked. I was glad he did; I was not concentrating properly on things I knew I should ask. The single cell with which the embryo began should split, and then each resultant cell should in turn split. One measure of the vigor and viability of an embryo is the number of its cells by the time of transfer.

'Yes, they were all two cells, except one I think was three. The ones we've left for transfer today are the best. They were both four cells but one was splitting again and may well be five by now.'

'That's great.' Lester took my hand. I asked: 'And do you know anything about these two–I mean, sex or anything?' At once I wondered why I had asked this, well aware that nothing at all could be gleaned from looking at the embryos except perhaps their relative 'quality' in the sense of likelihood of survival.

The lab technician, however, must have heard this mock-serious question many times before and patiently replied: 'I'm sure this one here must be a boy because it's giving me a lot of trouble–it won't come up into the pipette.' We laughed. 'Ah, now I've got them. Here you are then, you can look up at the screen now.'

There was our reward for having been good. Above our heads was a sight that no couple who fell pregnant naturally would ever see. We gazed up at our child–or children–at the very beginning of life. The two embryos were merely clear, rounded blobs of four cells each, a little like an anemone flower in shape and a jellyfish in texture. Yet I felt immediately and strongly a sense of their individuality, and a deep wondering about what each of them would be like if they managed to maintain life. Lester and I did not need to speak to know each other's awe and amazement.

'They're both good quality,' said the technician. 'You can see this one here is about to divide again: here two nuclei are forming in the one cell. And this other one shows plenty of movement of the matter inside each cell, too.'

'It's incredible. You know they're actually alive when you can see movement inside them.' There was swirling and swelling within the confines of each cell, an obvious struggle for life.

She laughed. 'Yes, I never really get tired of seeing them myself, and seeing people's reactions.'

'Can I look down the microscope as well?' I asked. Somehow I felt as though I'd be seeing a more realistic version of the embryos if they weren't on a screen—it was too much like a science documentary. I wanted to get closer to them.

'Sure.' So that's what I did, and stood watching them for about five minutes. Then Lester had a turn. We each wanted to stay quietly looking, but eventually the screen was switched off and the technician told me to prepare for the doctor, who would arrive in a moment. Once we were alone I partly undressed and sat on the bed with a sheet over my legs.

'How incredibly fantastic!' I exclaimed.

'I know. And soon they'll be with us.'

'How strange to think that we have four other babies that right now are frozen.'

The attending nurse that morning happened to be our favourite, Annette. She greeted us with an ample smile. 'How are the country bumpkins coping in the big smoke?'

'Sick of traffic lights, for one thing,' Lester replied.

'And how are you feeling?' she asked me.

71

'I haven't been too bad. You tend to forget how you're feeling in all the excitement.'

'I'm glad you're feeling excited. And I've got my fingers crossed for you.'

The lab technician re-appeared and, with her, our specialist, Dr Connell. He was an aloof, imposing man, the sort it was difficult to imagine doing anything ordinary or having a private life. He seemed to belong permanently in the hospital, like an indispensable piece of equipment. He briefly asked how we had found the cycle so far, and apologised for his lateness.

The transfer was quick and painless, like a smear test, merely a little clumsy. 'Now this is your mother talking,' I said as it proceeded. 'It's way past your bedtime.'

'Make yourself at home, babies,' added their father. The medical staff were concentrating so deeply that they did not react. Most likely they had heard such inane talk numerous times before. Finally the lab technician used the microscope to check the pipette that had held the embryos, to ensure that they had in fact been released.

We were then left alone for fifteen minutes and I was asked to lie relatively flat during this time. We had been given a cool drink each, and I tried to drink mine propped up on one elbow, without moving from the waist down. Lester and I grinned at each other.

'I suppose you'll have to move eventually, won't you?' he said.

'Yes, I don't know why I've got this ridiculous urge to stay right here for two weeks. They told us I could go about life normally and do everything short of going bungy-jumping, didn't they?'

'Terrible sacrifice. Not going bungy-jumping.'

'Mm.' I shifted to the other elbow, and sipped my drink. 'I mean, other women don't even know they're near a pregnancy, do they, and nobody goes around wrapped up in cotton wool.'

'No.'

Annette returned and verified with us our instructions for the remainder of the cycle, finishing with the obligatory 'good luck'.

Picture the return journey to Mum and Dad's. Anyone in the car with us would have thought that we were carrying an actual set of twins home from hospital.

'Well, babies,' began a typical speech. 'This is your car. We bought it especially because it's a nice big safe one and we hoped you'd be coming along one day.' Thus it continued, at intervals, throughout the half-hour journey. 'This is the city, where Grannie and Grandad live, but you'll be living on a farm – you'll see it in a few days' time. Now we're nearly at their house, and there's your little doggie, and there they are!'

The excitement had certainly not diminished the next day, although Mum and Dad did not show quite as much giggling foolishness – what had come over us? We had all planned a final Sunday lunch out, followed by a coast drive. I took my camera along and made them all pose, explaining that with any luck we would be able to look back on the resultant photos as 'baby's first outing.'

It was a beautiful day, and I was in high spirits and hopeful. The meal was delicious although I persisted in wanting mainly vegetables, as though my body was telling me what would do me the most good while I was still affected by drugs. I kept trying to remind myself that the injections of HCG I had to have would make me feel pregnant whether or not I was, and that it would take up to five days for an embryo to implant anyway. I must stay calm.

That evening Fiona telephoned, and I described the past few days. 'You must be on tenterhooks,' she said. 'How are you going to get through the next few weeks?'

'Strangely enough I'm quite looking forward to it all—I mean, I know the embryos are inside me and for as long as I know that I can be imagining how they've grown, and that they're okay. The part I'm dreading is the couple of days around when my period is due—that's when I think I'll be on tenterhooks.'

'Still okay for me to come down then?'

'Yes—absolutely.'

'You'll have someone to talk to about it other than Lester.'

'That's it. He's really good, though, really involved and loves talking about it. Anyway, bring rough clothes. We intend to make use of you.'

Several people at the clinic had said that the next two weeks would be the longest in our lives, but this was not our experience. Once home we found ourselves short of time. Working hard, particularly catching up on a backlog of farm jobs due to the time spent away, we felt as usual that there were not enough hours in the day to do all that we should.

I deliberately took time, and care, to monitor my health. I read the descriptions in the IVF patient handbook of the symptoms of ovarian hyperstimulation syndrome, a danger at this stage of the cycle. To avoid it I drank a great deal of water, as was recommended. I tucked into fruits, vegetables, nuts and wholegrains, napped when I could, and continued to sacrifice my nightly glass of wine.

I had thought before undergoing this first IVF transfer that I would not limit myself physically once I returned to work. However at home I detected a subtle change in attitude in myself, a greater protectiveness towards my own body. I know they said to go about normal life, I thought, but I do so much more on the farm than many women would, and perhaps I ought to tone it down a little. So I shied away, in many small ways over the course of a day, from heavy work.

While my body was not fully on the job, as indeed it had not been for some time, neither was my mind focused on work. I found myself thinking constantly about what was happening inside me. On impulse, on two separate occasions, I bought books pertaining to pregnancy. I'd never even noticed shelves of baby books in bookshops until recently, having always made a beeline for travel or fiction. One of the books was a factual, cover-every-aspect-of-the-topic manual, and the other was an awe-inspiring collection of photographs of the growing foetus in utero. I read and re-read passages of these books. I found myself wanting to know what made some embryos implant while others failed to do so, and was disappointed to find that in fact there was very little I could hope to know about this since even the experts acknowledged their lack of understanding.

I hoped, prayed, made bargains with God: 'Let the babies survive and I'll be far more tolerant of people.'

I constantly imagined the stage of development of the

embryos, and was very excited ten days into the waiting period to read that by now the embryos would actually be large enough to be visible to the naked eye. While I stood helping Lester, who was mending a fence, I looked at freckles on my skin. I chose one that I thought would be about the size of the embryos by now and showed it to Lester. He, too, was excited, but his mind was on work.

Only at the end of the day did Lester allow himself to indulge in imaginative talk with me about the babies, and when we were in bed at night the two of us would lie, one hand each on my stomach, talking to the babies and willing them to stay. It was as if we were already pregnant, and I was amazed at how overwhelming and obsessive a feeling it was, and that I already loved the offspring inside me.

'Do you think we're letting ourselves talk like this too much?' I asked Lester. 'We might fall in love with the babies and feel even worse that way if we lose them. Maybe we should just try and forget that they're there.'

'How? How are we supposed to do that? And we'd feel bad anyway if we lost them, regardless of how much we've talked to them. Let's enjoy the moment while we can.'

Every minute of the day became an opportunity for my imagination to wander. Lingering over a shower with grooming tasks that were more indulgent than urgent, I found myself thinking: how am I going to manage to do this with a toddler around? Wait until Lester sits down to relax and can be watching the child at the same time, I suppose. I was crossing the home paddock to tie up and feed the working dogs, they knocking one another over in their excitement: hm, one of those backpack baby carriers would definitely be useful, I mused.

Stitching while half-watching a movie, my legs propped across Lester's legs, I imagined a voice: 'Mummy, I want a drink,' and looked up to see a pyjama-clad mite standing at the passage door.

My heart's hope was a girl, to share with her the joys of *Little Women*, *Heidi*, *Rilla of Ingleside*, and shopping.

There was neither trepidation nor resistance to change in these daydreams; rather, a sense of wonder at the capacity of life to take another course, just when I thought that my lifestyle had been decided.

I indulged constantly, obsessively, in imaginings in which I announced my pregnancy to family and friends, picturing the when, where, and how, and the joyful reactions.

Liz rang during this waiting time, and was filled in on how the time in the city had been spent. Then I changed the subject to the one that was most on my mind. 'How early did you know you were pregnant?' I took the opportunity to ask, fishing for a reply in which I might recognise some symptom that I was experiencing. But she laughed and said that she couldn't really remember. Her mind was on the present day, present lives.

'James had a fall – or rather a push – at school today and had to have stitches.'

'Poor boy!' I asked for the details, commiserated and let her go, asking her to give him a hug from me.

Mum and Dad rang repeatedly. 'Do you feel any different?' seemed to be Mum's favourite question.

'Well, Mum, it's hard to say. I do feel different to how I would normally, but then I'm full of drugs, so who's to say whether it's pregnancy or the drugs making me feel that way? Anyway, we'll keep you informed, and if nothing has happened by Saturday we'll plan to head up on Sunday for that blood test. Fiona's arriving Thursday, on the bus, so we'll bring her back with us if we're coming. Otherwise she's happy to get the bus back. I'm sorry we can't be more precise about whether or not we'll be with you.'

'Don't worry about that. Take care and stay rested. We'll hope to see you, but just you remember what I've been saying all along. Your father and I want this pregnancy for your sake, not ours – we just want what you want.'

'Thanks, Mum. Thanks for that. Unless you hear from us Sunday morning, we'll be on our way then.'

Soon only a few days remained until the Saturday when my period was due. I would almost wish to stop time from moving ahead, to stay on this peak from where I could see so many possibilities. But this quasi-pregnancy had to either become reality, or come to an end.

Chapter Ten

On the Thursday afternoon I collected Fiona from the bus depot.

Her visit was fun. Very much a city person, Fiona made continual mock-scathing observations about this peculiar farm life that I had chosen, and kept me permanently giggling. It was a welcome distraction from waiting. I felt tired, as usual lately, and unable to entertain Fiona in the way that I would have liked, but I knew that in this friendship it did not matter.

Saturday morning came and went with no sign of a period, except some warning cramps. But, unusually, they passed, and it gave me a firmer belief in the possibility that I might be pregnant.

I drove Fiona to our other block to show her around there and check the stock. But I did not apply myself to my observations as I usually would. 'To think that I might be pregnant at this very moment!' I kept thinking—and repeatedly saying—in my distraction. I wasn't paying a great deal of attention to Fiona's descriptions of her travels, which ordinarily I would have loved to hear.

'I know, it's really exciting,' Fiona would patiently reply, and search for some way of displaying more enthusiasm. 'I used to know how to knit—I'll have to brush up on it and make you something.'

I hadn't really heard. 'But I won't feel safe until a few days more have passed. I'm in two minds about going up to town tomorrow. I bet as soon as we arrive I'll get my period.'

But I was convinced that I was going to need a pregnancy test. In the kitchen was a dresser where, whenever a trip was imminent, Lester and I would place anything we would need to take, as it came to mind. On it now stood a number of items ready to go.

Later that afternoon I experienced a little spotting, and my heart plummeted. But I remembered having read somewhere that this can happen even in pregnancy around the time when a period would be due. So I calmed myself and allowed my hopes to rise again. I told Lester and Fiona, however. My friend took my arm, sympathetic. Lester hid any concern that he might be feeling, and referred to practical details. 'You'd better ring your mother, darling, and tell her that we may not be coming.'

It helped to do so, anyway. Mum told me that she'd had spotting when first pregnant and not to give up hope yet.

'But Mum, all the effort, and I'll feel terrible for your sake after the way you helped us.'

'I've told you—forget about us. Just take care and don't worry yourself.' So I continued to enjoy the high, while I could, and to let images of us with a child skip across my mind.

That night I lay down happy, well and with preparations for the trip of a lifetime underway. Lying sleepily listening to the neighbour's ewes calling their newly weaned lambs, I realised that there were still some people whom I had not imagined telling yet. So I did that before sleeping.

At around one I woke. I had strong stomach pain and without even going to the bathroom to check, I knew. I knew that two children had died.

I dare say that I had lived a fortunate, cosseted life thus far. I had never known that emotions could plummet from one extreme to the other on a near-vertical gradient.

I had known sadness, of course, but it had always crept up and whispered until I knew it was there. Or, if it came suddenly, it contrasted with contentment, not elation. Now I went from the joyous pinnacle that was belief in my pregnancy to the flat depths, robbed of my joy in one sickening and fearful slide.

My babies were dead. They may have already passed out of me like so much waste. No help to tell myself that this happened countless times to other women, and that they didn't even know. I did know, and it hurt.

I snuggled my stomach against Lester's back so that his warmth could ease my cramps. I often did this, with his blessing. This time it woke him, and at once he knew too. He turned and held me, and I cried and cried. We grieved together.

I had never, not once in my life, known such knock-down-flat disappointment. Upsets, yes. Missing people, yes. Temporary setbacks, loneliness, envy, hankering, fatigue, discouragement, yes. But never such disappointment. It was beyond my understanding, somehow, that Lester and I could have mounted so much effort over the past months, and failed. The logistics of liaising with a clinic so far away, sending blood tests there, taking drugs, organising absence from the farm and keeping our secret, had all come to nothing. Until now, amount of effort had always determined degree of success, in whatever field of life – if you wanted something you simply gave whatever effort was necessary to achieve it. For both Lester and I that seemed to go without saying. How could we want something so much, have done all that we could, and failed?

I had to say goodbye to all the dear pictures that had been crowding my mind. It was a strange, elusive form of grief. I had never really had that which I now felt so deeply I had lost. The sudden reversal of emotions was a huge tremor emanating from the very core of me, a fearful force scattering the fantasy beings that had been inhabiting my secret corners.

I tried to tell this to Lester – hesitantly, for the emotions were so unfamiliar and I hadn't communicated to him anything of the way that I had been living in my imagination. I didn't know whether he had been doing the same, and whether this had intensified his loss, too. I asked him how he felt. I'd turned to him for my comfort, which he always gave amply, but he must have crashed as well.

'I'd seen it coming with what you told me this afternoon,' he said, stroking my head.

'But you were still talking to the babies when we went to bed.'

'Yes. Keeping the happiness there until we knew for sure. But I didn't really expect to succeed the first time.'

'I guess I kidded myself nothing was wrong after this afternoon.'

'That's only natural.'

'Hope springs eternal.'

'Yes.'

'I don't even know what's happened to my mind the last couple of weeks. The babies have been on it the whole time and the more I've thought about them the more I've wanted them and the harder it's been to stop thinking about them and be sensible.'

'That's just all the love you have to give.'

That made me cry some more, until I was tired enough to sleep. On the Sunday morning more tears had to flow. I rang my parents as early as possible, in order not to prolong their anticipation. This was so very hard to do. Not only had I never known disappointment myself, but I'd rarely had to be the cause of it to my parents, and did not like the feeling. We had involved them – it had been a case of necessity – and encouraged them to hope, but had set them up for a fall. As I spoke to my mother I could sense that something had been quelled in her, too, even though Mum could not have been kinder. It was a short call, Mum trying to do the talking as I sobbed.

'We're sad for you, my dear, not for ourselves. What we hope for is that you can accept and cope with whatever is going to happen, and move on from it in whatever way you choose.'

'Yes, it's just all the incredible effort that's come to nothing. And two lives have gone. I can't think of them as just embryos. They were unique.'

'I know. This is what's going to be hardest for you to deal with. But don't forget that other women lose embryos many times before they achieve a pregnancy, and they don't even know it.'

'I'm aware of that.'

'Anyway, look after yourself today and we'll give you another ring tonight. Have you told Fiona yet?'

'No, she's not up yet. I was just going to take her in a cup of tea soon.'

'Right. Well, you enjoy the last part of your visit with her. We love you and we're thinking of you. Don't lose heart.'

The tears dried from this conversation, but then it was time to go to the spare room, wake Fiona and tell her.

'Oh, no, how awful!' she said, rising quickly, taking me to a chair and putting me in it with her arm around me. 'After everything you've had to do!'

She was upset for me, but not along with me: the extent of my pain was surprising even myself, and I could not expect her to fathom this. To me there were lives involved, to anyone else I suppose it was just the equivalent of a failed attempt to achieve: on a par with a poor job interview, an impossible exam, an auction at which you see the home that you want go to someone else. Before I started IVF I'd assumed that this was the way I'd feel, too. Now I was thinking of children, at different stages of their lives, who would have been and who never would be.

We made the mistake of going to church, following plans made earlier. Once there, already red-eyed and miserable, I was unable to stop the tears welling as I felt the contrast between myself and the calm faces around me.

The congregation stood to sing a hymn, but I could not join in. I sat, weeping, instead, and listened angrily and unreceptively.

Breathe through the heat of our desire
Thy coolness and thy balm
Let sense be dumb, let flesh retire,
Speak through the earthquake, wind and fire,
O still small voice of calm.

Words that until now had always seemed gentle and poetic suddenly teased.

Never mind that the rest of the visit had been so enjoyable, I wished that my friend were no longer there as we returned to the house. Three hours to go until we had to take Fiona to the bus. I wished I could be alone, or alone with Lester, and lie numb on the bed until I felt better. Instead I had to make some conversation, and a midday meal, and not embarrass my guest too much with my misery. But that was unfair. Fiona shared my grief, and wanted it gone, and had much to say to ease it:

'You only need it to work once.'

'I have a feeling that the next cycle will be the one.'

'You're no quitter.'

But at last we were alone. I would ring Liz, the only other person with whom I felt I could share the news, in a few days' time. Lester would ring his mother soon, no doubt. One other phone call had to be made, though, and that was to the clinic. Knowing that I would break down again if I had to do this myself, I asked Lester to ring, and sat with him as he did so. It was Annette who answered. 'You poor things!' she said with genuine feeling. 'How is Julia?'

'She's pretty cut up,' Lester replied.

'Yes, after all this has involved for you, so far away. I know you won't want to think about this straight away, but if you want to book on for another drug cycle it's best to do so well ahead. But we'll ring in a week or so to see how you're feeling and what you've decided.'

I headed for bed early and found a card on my pillow, from Lester. It had a photo of a puppy that was exactly like Murray when he had been younger. Lester had written comforting words of love, sympathy and encouragement. He had to have bought the card days ago, when we were last at the shops, in case I needed it.

Chapter Eleven

We were shortly, strangely, happy again. The usual challenges of life were mere undulations after that one, terrible slump. There'd been some upsets – facing a crowd at shearing, mainly – but I hadn't dreamed of such an early recovery of my equilibrium. There was now plenty to occupy our thoughts, since Christmas was coming, as were all the family, and meanwhile we had work to do – allocate rams to ewes, cart hay, and drench.

One day, in particular, I was struck by the contrast between life on an IVF cycle and normal life. I was about to start the day by mustering. Lester was already at the shearing-shed, where he would make a start on the drenching after shifting some ewes around. Like any job on sheep it's not the work itself that's time-consuming but the preparations for it, and the movement of the stock. Some of the mobs had been at the shed for days now and needed to be let out for a feed and a drink in the small holding paddocks. It takes time, much time, to let mobs out and later to fit them back into the shed, but long experience had taught Lester that it is more efficient to have as many mobs around as possible and to work on them intensively. Experience had also taught him that those big lowering thunderheads that had been hanging around us for days would break and make the sheep very soggy and uncomfortable to work on. So he'd kept as many as possible under cover.

We'd put in a solid day here the day before, drenching merinos. This day we'd one mob of merinos left – a hundred and fifty – then a mob of five hundred and seventy lambs. Neither of us was looking forward to the little wrigglers. Then all the crossbred ewes: five mobs, one of which was the mob I was about to muster. And I knew that Lester had in mind to do all the 'odd' mobs – the studs, the pets, the killers, the rams.

I'd asked: 'We can leave the little mobs until tomorrow I suppose?', knowing that he'd say that no, he wanted to start hay-carting tomorrow.

'No, we'll be hay-carting. We've got a lot to do if you want to go for another cycle straight after Christmas.'

Okay, a fourteen-hour day. So be it. We'd feel a sense of accomplishment by the end of it, anyway.

It's seven in the morning now, the best time of the day for shifting sheep. Cool air wafts across Laddie and I as we ride the motorbike, the sun is glinting low between the branches of the redgums and sheep are mobile as they graze, so they will not have to be forced up from their 'camps'. There's a white lake on the horizon, a mirage formed of sunlit fog, with wattle masts and sails. We're having frisky-fresh mornings and evenings this late spring, glow-warm noons.

I feel alive. So grateful to be active again, as though I've been imprisoned for weeks and have regained my freedom.

Full of the simple joy of having my mind focused on a task that I can complete. I love mustering: the partnership with the working dog, the chance for some thinking time while we follow the mob.

If you've ever seen a mob of sheep being mustered, you'll have wondered what invisible shifting substance is surrounding the collective shape and guiding its liquid movement. What could make hundreds of animals, not particularly bright but with a definite will of their own, go exactly where one human being and a dog want them to go? The sheep are scattered everywhere as they forage for that clover plant, that juicy stalk where the dew collects. Laddie drops from the bike and the arc of his run nets the sheep: his instinct to push them, theirs to gather in safe numbers. In no time they're a mass of woolly bodies pouring through a gate into a laneway like sand through a funnel.

I relax: the mob all caught, it's just a matter of following them to the shed, a pleasant ten-minute bike ride.

Seven-forty: Lester's drenched a mob by the time I arrive at the shed with the sheep. 'Do you want me to drench with you, or take these away?'

'Take them away while it's cool, if you like.'

Eight-fifteen: I return to the shed. Lester's on the lambs, and grateful for a hand. He works from the front of the race to the back, and I do the opposite. We each thrust one knee against an animal to jam it against those in front, bring the left hand around the jaw of the unsuspecting lamb, wiggle the nozzle of the drench gun between its teeth. One squirt, which makes the animal toss its head, spit or cough.

It's more difficult for Lester at the front, because all the lambs are able to see him coming. They can plan their dodging tactics, and play us up something terrible: leaping out of our grasp, stamping on us, climbing onto one another's backs and scrambling out of the race, ducking behind us to join those already drenched. We turn around to be faced by a trio of bums and wonder, 'Now, which one didn't get done?' We meet in the middle of the race. 'Have you done him?' – with a point of the gun. 'Yes, but not the two underneath him.'

Each time that we empty the drenching race and go into the shed for more sheep, I look at the remaining lambs and calculate: 'Looks like five more racefuls,' 'Two to go,' and so on.

I'm enjoying myself – despite the sore toes, the dust of the yard, my sweat and the prickles in the sheep. My body is strong and I rejoice in the challenge of handling each animal. My mind is engaged in planning the order in which I'll return mobs and set up gates on the way for the next mob.

I haven't thought about IVF for days, I realise. Who was that person, a few weeks ago, whose mind veiled over with a film of longing?

'What are you grinning for?' Lester asks, as we meet in the middle of a raceful. 'You do realise we'll be here until eight tonight?' He thinks I'm mad, looking happy while nine hundred sheep are looking at us.

How to explain it: that I don't feel passive. That I'm strong and capable again. I pull his hat down over his eyes instead.

Chapter Twelve

We tried again early in January, a frozen cycle.

We had overcome our disappointment and were full of positive anticipation. Our thoughts had turned to the four babies waiting for us, alive but with their growth suspended. The miracle of IVF would work for us soon, and I had a feeling that it would be on one of these natural cycles, when my body could function free from interference. Once again we were looking forward to doing, to actively moving ahead towards our goal.

Not that there was a great deal to do. Compared to the demands placed on us the previous October, this was a breeze. In fact, because the cycle had an entirely different feel, it was easy to forget that a momentous experience was again about to happen. All that I had to do was make a phone call to the clinic to book on and have two blood samples taken, one on a day when I happened to be shopping in the local town anyway, and one in another country hospital on the way to the city. These would show the day for embryo transfer, which we were told would be around the twelfth day of my natural cycle, enabling us to plan a date for our trip. We were to take the two bloods into the clinic with us the morning after our arrival. There were no drugs to take, no injections to administer.

As for organisation of the farm, this was a time of year when, naturally, there was work that we could be doing—spreading gravel, cleaning troughs—but when we would tend to take a short break anyway. So we planned our city visit in a holiday mood. We merely had to ask a neighbour to keep an eye on the windmills and feed the working dogs. We would only be away for a few days and it wasn't worth employing anyone. Fire was always a concern at this time of year, but luckily the forecast was for cool weather.

The procedure for the cycle was that my natural hormone levels would be monitored so that two days after I had ovulated the clinic would thaw and transfer two embryos, mirroring natural optimum fertilisation time as closely as possible. Then I would be sent home to wait for two weeks. There would be no drug support at this stage, either.

It was good that the cycle was not at all involved. The smaller our emotional outlay, the less I would be expecting back, and success would come all the more easily for a relaxed attitude. I felt that I had made a grave mistake last time in my excited imaginings. I'd invested too much emotion in the process, let myself get too attached to the babies. This time I would be much more pragmatic and would not even think about what was going to happen. The less contact we had to have with the clinic, the easier this would be. I knew that the process would work soon if I stayed calm.

At first it was easy to maintain the detachment that I

sought. The city visit seemed much like any other that we had made in the past, before our involvement with IVF. I behaved as though Lester and I were merely taking a few days' break with my parents, but that I happened to have to keep one or two medical appointments during the visit, equivalent in tiresomeness and lack of importance to a trip to the dentist.

On the morning after our arrival we drove in to deliver the two bloods and to have a third sample taken, hoping they would show the rising oestrogen levels associated with ovulation. As we entered the clinic I managed to think ahead to our next destination—the shops—and to refuse to be reminded of our earlier cycle, or to be anything less than buoyant. The blood test over, I was drawn to the sales and the food markets

We managed to fit in all the social activities we had planned and still spend a casual few days as we waited for the embryo transfer. My parents and Lester bombarded me with not-very-veiled hints that I should be resting quietly, but I knew that I could combine treatment with making the most of being in town. I enjoyed preparing lunch on the Saturday for some friends. Feeling so fit and relaxed, I could temporarily forget the real reason for our presence in the city.

The transfer, as it turned out, was scheduled for the Sunday. The previous afternoon I rang the clinic and was told that three embryos had had to be thawed, as one had not survived the thawing process, and that the two survivors were currently each of two cells. We were disappointed at this loss, but not grieving, although somehow I felt as though I should be.

As we drove to the clinic on the Sunday morning I still felt quite unconvinced of the fact that we were involved in a cycle. The previous October the drugs and injections had been constant reminders, the fourteen days after transfer were to be counted away. This time my mind was not on the waiting period, nor on the all-important date two weeks from today, but on the fact that we wanted to return to the city in a week's time—Fiona had invited us to a party—and on how we were going to manage to leave the farm again.

My preoccupations and my self-command vanished as we arrived at the clinic. Or, rather, at the very moment of embryo transfer, until which point something in me had steadfastly refused excitement, snubbed significance.

But the technician would have to go and put those embryos up on the screen again, wouldn't she? And one of them would have to have grown quite spectacularly since the day before.

There it was, eight cells, struggling for life, and I had to realise that I couldn't avoid being deeply affected once again. I looked at this embryo, loved it for its growth, felt a stab within me at the thought that it may not grow any more, and burst into tears.

The technician displaying the embryo on the screen was quite concerned. 'What's the matter—aren't you well?'

Lester was trying to console me and not be too moved himself by my display of emotion.

'It's all right. She's just moved by the sight of the embryo.' He hugged my shoulders. 'Come on, enjoy the moment with me.'

'It's so beautiful and strong, and it may not live.'

'But it might.'

I managed to stop crying before the doctor and sister came in, but they too were most solicitous. The doctor, in particular, seemed puzzled. 'Has someone said or done something to upset you?' she asked.

'No, no …' I was crying again at the kindness. 'It's just the sight of the embryos, and we failed last time.'

The other embryo to be inserted was only two cells, and looked slightly fragmented. Something in my mind was attaching itself to the strong, larger embryo, and endowing it, ridiculously, with character traits of persistence and perseverance for having so successfully survived freezing and thawing. I blubbered on while the transfer took place, no doubt making it very difficult for those involved.

We were left alone for fifteen minutes of peace and quiet. I had entered that room in control of my emotions and with a balanced attitude to a full life. I knew that I was going to leave it completely obsessed, not with the idea of pregnancy in general, but with that of these particular embryos taking.

As we left the clinic, I was crying still with frustration at the inevitable emotional pull. No matter how I imagined I would like to react to IVF, strange emotions that I had never known in earlier life somehow took over. I thought I had been happy before, but now it seemed like an ignorant, inferior sort of happiness.

If anyone had told me, say, ten years before, that I would become virtually one-track-minded about pregnancy, I would never have believed them. Mine was not a mind that had left much room for babies. But during the time in which we were waiting for a result, I thought of little else than the embryos inside me, whether or not they would implant, and my visions of everything that would ensue if they did. I woke each day and happily remembered my secret possibility, carrying it with me through the hours. It was the same satisfactory feeling as approaching any milestone in life toward which you have been journeying. The sort of uplifted feeling you carry in your teens when you pass your exams, or later when you fall in love, when you buy a home, when you earn a promotion ... life is happening!

And I wasn't just imagining. By the end of the first week (by which time we were in the city again for Fiona's party) I had a firm belief that at least one of the embryos had implanted. I felt different. Had suffered twinges, nausea, pains—and this time there were no drugs to explain any of them. It was in great contrast to my normal, uneventful month. Was I kidding myself, feeling what I wanted to feel? Not at all.

At the party I wanted desperately to tell Fiona how I'd been feeling. I was avoiding telling Lester, in case I raised his hopes for nothing: as strong as my conviction was, I knew that an implantation could easily be followed by an early miscarriage. But someone had to know.

Fiona and her guests were seated round the garden, so that it was difficult to talk privately. I had to ask her for a non-alcoholic drink, rather than the punch that was being offered, in order to get her alone in the kitchen. I described to her what I'd been feeling.

'That's great! I told you I had a premonition that this would be the one that works.'

'I hope you're right. I'm so excited. I just want this baby— these babies—so much.'

'And you who had never shown any interest in babies

before. You never want to hold anyone else's baby or look at them in a pram, do you? You've really surprised me in how strong your feelings obviously are.'

'But these babies are different. These are mine!'

Fiona was wonderful. She let me bore her for quite some time with details of my bodily developments. I was becoming fascinated by anything medical. I hoped that this wouldn't lead me to become one of those mothers who describe their children's illnesses in great detail to anyone who'll listen.

And Lester? In some ways his role during the two weeks of waiting was more difficult than mine. I at least could watch for signs, would be the one who would first be aware of changes. He was living the situation too, but in a no-doubt frustratingly passive way. He worked hard through the rest of that week, supported me with talk, practical help and affection, and waited, inscrutable, not demanding anything of me.

Later in the second week I had a sign that my period was on the way. I began to spot four days before the due date. It was what I had been dreading, and although it wasn't a sure sign that I wasn't pregnant, something told me that the inevitable was going to happen.

The cycle did fail.

Another card appeared on my pillow. It was a gesture of empathy, a hand to steady me, but the fact that Lester had prepared for failure by buying the card brought home to me a difference in our respective experiences. He was better able than me to see that the process wasn't going to be easy. He could be more stoic and prepare for the falls because he was ever so slightly removed from the process. If he had been carrying the embryos, perhaps he would have ridden to greater heights of hope with me.

Added to my sorrow, this time, was anger, a cheated feeling, and confusion. The one embryo in particular had seemed to clamour for a chance at life, and I would always believe that it had begun to implant. Therefore, something had gone wrong in the last few days of my cycle. Why? Was there something wrong with me? At first I felt useless, old, discouraged.

And yet anger can be positive, can be turned to determination. I wanted all the more that which we had come so close to having. Two cycles was not a great deal to have gone through, and we would learn from them, make some changes, and succeed next time. I told myself: 'I think I can.'

Chapter Thirteen

The next cycle was going to have to be stimulated. We did have one remaining frozen embryo, but since the likelihood of success of a frozen cycle was much less than that of a drug cycle, it seemed to make more sense to leave that embryo where it was until we could add others to it. We might go to all the trouble of leaving the farm and the embryo not thaw successfully.

I was now in circumstances in which the clinic would allow me to have three embryos transferred, in order to increase the chances of success. No fixed rule of age alone determined these circumstances; your tally of unsuccessful procedures was also a factor. We decided to take advantage of this, if we were lucky enough to obtain enough embryos. To try for three on our first cycle would have been foolish – if we'd been 'IVF compatible' we could have found ourselves with triplets. Now, after two failures, triplets did not seem at all likely.

Given, then, that we were looking at a lengthy drug cycle, we needed to find a timeslot in the farm calendar during which we would be able to leave. This proved difficult, mid-year. If IVF had not been a part of our lives, the only times when we would have gone away would have been during August, when the paddocks are too wet to cross without getting bogged and when we would usually head north seeking sunshine, the Christmas break, when we would spend a few days at the sea, and a weekend here and there. Throughout the rest of the year the farm claimed not only our energy for hard work, but our presence for the well-being of the stock. In summer, to look at wind-mills daily and to guard against fires. In autumn, to feed hungry stock and monitor calving cows. In winter, to daily check lambing ewes. In spring, to ensure that cross-bred ewes heavy with damp wool did not go down and fail to get up again. We'd risked a spring drug cycle the first time and employed help on the farm, but there were only so many people whom we could ask to keep doing our work for us. Everyone nearby had their own farms to worry about.

We looked at the calendar, looked at the list of jobs, nutted out priorities, and seriously considered ditching the whole project. February was out: too hot, too dry, and too soon after the frozen cycle. March—we had workers coming in for crutching. April—we had our usual mob of old ewes lambing, and cows calving. May—definitely out: main lambing would begin.

April seemed the lesser evil. I could be on the drugs through March, the old sheep shouldn't have too much trouble lambing, most of the cows should have finished calving, and Lester had thought of a neighbour's lad who would enjoy the responsibility of checking our stock on his own. It went very much against the grain with us to leave the farm when there were stock giving birth, but the alternative seemed too long a wait.

And so April it was. I determined, this time, to learn by what had seemed to be mistakes. I would concentrate on IVF and leave socialising for another time. I would keep a level head, seeing not vistas of the future but only the challenging climb immediately ahead of us.

We had the drugs sent to us and carried out the injections with the savoir-faire of trained medicos. All went well with the cycle. Mum and Dad welcomed us unhesitatingly and shared in our mounting anticipation. My egg pick-up was delayed, but successful—eleven eggs collected. We were slightly disappointed that only six fertilised, but cheered ourselves with the thought that it still gave us enough for a transfer of three and a frozen cycle later, if need be.

On the day of the embryo transfer I was lighthearted, positive and resolved to participate joyfully. It was once again intensely moving to see the three chosen embryos on the screen, but I mastered my emotions this time. Lester and I had decided to stay at the clinic as long as possible after the transfer, and in fact I remained lying on the bed for almost three-quarters of an hour after the nurse and doctor had left, just trying to give the babies every chance to take hold, even though I knew this may not happen for days if at all.

This effort at extreme care and caution persisted for many days to follow. 'Shall we take the dogs to the beach before we have to go home?' Lester suggested one beautiful, hot morning.

'You go—I'm sitting right here until I get in the car to go home. We can go to the beach anytime once we know I'm pregnant.' But I could sense that Lester was bored, and anxious to return home now that our 'business' was finished.

Once again those now familiar feelings of hope thawed within me. Somehow, until embryo transfer had taken place it was easy to remain rational and aware that all the effort would as likely as not come to nothing. It was easy not to get your hopes up, to remain focused on other plans and aspects of your life.

But once those embryos were part of you, a desperate one-eyed craving took over and sweet imaginings took the place of everyday concerns. I wanted not any pregnancy but the life of the personalities within me. Some hitherto little-used part of my mind had seemingly taken over. It was the exquisite pain of wishing, like waiting for a new lover to call.

I felt a daily compulsion to re-read written descriptions of how large the embryos would be by now. I watched my body, emotions and mind for any signs of differences and new developments. I played mental re-runs of those pregnancy announcement scenes, planned schedules once the baby or babies arrived, pictured scenes in the child's development: how we'd amuse the child during long car journeys, how to teach table manners, what the teacher would say after the first day of school, and what I'd reply.

Lester and I had decided that this time we would not put ourselves through the pain of being on the verge of a trip to the city for a pregnancy test, only to have to change our plans. We would wait until at least three days after the expected date of my period before leaving. Embryo transfer had been on a Friday, so my period was due on a Friday. Friday came and went, and I had had no indication of an imminent period. Again I had felt unusual nausea and sensations within myself, and dared to really hope, and once the dreaded Friday had passed, hope turned to triumph. On the Saturday, I experienced some strong pain that would normally indicate the beginning of flow, but it disappeared, and this only encouraged me.

That day I rang my parents to let them know that so far all was well. If my period had not arrived by Monday morning, I told them, Lester and I were prepared to make the trip.

Over the course of the weekend our anticipation mounted to the point where it required an extreme effort to think about anything at all other than the possibility that we might finally be pregnant. We waited as late as mid-morning on the Monday. Lester returned from fixing an electric wire, and came into the house with an expression that was half hope, half apprehension.

'Are we still going?' he asked.

'Yes!'

'Right. I'd better pack.'

The talk in the car on the journey was all as if the pregnancy had already been confirmed: plans, details, arrangements, necessities, jokes, names, dates, feelings, pleasures. This doubled once we arrived and Grandma and Grandad joined in the conversation, too.

The fact that I was now four days late convinced us all of the fact that this must be the long-awaited pregnancy. We couldn't wait until the test the following day. Nobody seemed to want to talk about anything else. I had experienced more nausea in the car but it had passed, and I assumed it must be the beginnings of morning sickness.

Dad suggested a pub meal that night, as this was a relatively unplanned visit and Mum wasn't prepared for a meal for four. The choice was an 'all you can eat' bar. I couldn't eat a great deal, however, and watched as the others devoured my money's worth. I replaced my fork and my right hand went to my abdomen. 'Did you get much morning sickness, when you were pregnant?' I asked my mother while Dad and Lester were away re-heaping their plates. I was quite ready to begin on the experience of comparing my pregnancy with other women's.

'Hardly any at all. Why – are you feeling sick again?'

'Probably over-excited, too. I'll never sleep tonight. I wish I could nave gone straight to the clinic for the test.'

We weren't late back to the house. By this time I felt so nauseous that I went straight to the toilet. What I discovered there crushed me under a weight so huge that I was incapable of moving for fully five minutes. I suddenly understood an expression – 'emotional rollercoaster' that I had heard so often used in connection with IVF. From the high of hope, then of conviction that I was pregnant, with all the glistening images that accompanied it, I was catapulted to something that the word 'disappointment' was woefully inadequate to describe. All the anticipation of telling this, that and the other person vanished. All the decisions about what to buy, how to decorate the room and how to care for the new baby were redundant. All the pictures of my children died. My children themselves died, my children of two weeks I knew had been inside me. And I had to face disappointing my beloved husband and parents, whom even now, a few metres away, I could hear talking happily about the expansion of the family. Of course, these were all the same emotions I'd endured after the first failure, but in the intervening months I'd allowed myself to forget them. Now they could hit me hard.

I walked into the lounge, not crying yet, and stood waiting while somebody, I did not register who, was speaking. They were all looking at me, and Lester asked, 'What's up?'

I just replied, 'I'm sorry, everybody.'

'Oh, Julia, I thought this was going to happen when you said you were feeling sick at tea,' said Mum.

Lester looked destroyed. But he rose, put his arm around me and led me to the privacy of our bedroom. That's when I began sobbing. 'I can't do this any more. I just can't. It's too hard and I'm not doing it any more.'

'I know. Not now, though.'

'I can't. I can't do it again. It's too awful having the babies.'

I sobbed like this for twenty minutes. I felt as though I'd failed everybody, particularly Lester. 'If you want to find somebody else who can have babies easily, I'll understand,' I said.

'WHAT?' he erupted, and then made an effort to calm himself and speak quietly. 'Don't ever say things like that. You are my partner for life, this is our problem, and if we end up childless, I still want to be with you. Right?'

I nodded.

'In any case,' he added, 'who's to say there isn't something wrong with me as well?'

I looked at him as I blew my nose. I realised that he was feeling as inadequate as I was. 'I suppose, but we don't know that.' The focus had always been on my body, but our failures could be due to other factors, unknown to us, that had to do with Lester's health. This was part of what was so hard to take at the moment – our failures were all unexplained.

Lester suggested that we sit with Mum and Dad. Everyone's mood had changed abruptly, but my parents' concern, despite their own disappointment, was for our obvious distress.

'I wouldn't blame you one bit if you felt you couldn't go on with this,' Mum said.

'I don't know what I want to do. I know I don't want to put you through this any more. Nobody else has to put their parents through this: getting your hopes up and then wrecking them all in one day.'

'Don't you be silly. We'll back you up whatever you decide to do. We just want you to be happy.'

We tried again in September. Three frozen embryos awaited their chance at survival. Neither Lester nor I held any great hope for the cycle, but we could not move on, in whatever way we were to do so, without using those embryos. We could not just forget them, or have them disposed of.

All three thawed successfully. None implanted.

And another card appeared on my pillow.

Chapter Fourteen

I lay awake while Lester slept soundly. All the pressure, all of it, was on me. Did I want to give up? Had I had enough? A decision needed to be made about whether we wanted to investigate a new treatment on offer interstate.

Let's be honest. There probably wasn't much point in seeing any other doctors. I would only go through with it, it seemed to me, because it was too soon to quit or because I owed it to others. I even began to question whether I myself wanted a child any more or whether I would prefer to come back to life—my own life. There were still imagined scenes of maternal fulfilment. But there were just as many in which I happily directed my energies elsewhere. I hated the thought of more pointless tests, more intrusions and the effort of beginning the whole round again.

Lester, typically, maddeningly, had not been willing to enter into any conflict about the issue. 'It's up to you,' or 'I'll leave it in your hands,' was all he would say. The trouble was that he said it with suddenly saddened eyes, leaving me in no doubt that he hadn't yet abandoned hope or reached the point where he wanted to stop trying. If he would only say clearly that he wanted to continue, so that the pressure that he was putting on me could be definite and obvious. But no, irreproachability was his forte.

You would think it never entered Lester's head. Every night he'd slept soundly, while I'd plunged into dark pools of emotions and fished there for that slippery, elusive prey: a reasonable decision. Just as I was doing this night.

I remembered how quickly, in fact, I'd rallied after the first failure, when the anguish had been deep, but not prolonged. When Lester and I had mourned the loss of the babies, and often expressed this to each other. When my logical mind had told me that it is only in rare cases that the first IVF cycle succeeds, that we may have to try several times, and that I would need to find great strength to do so.

I'd clearly allowed enthusiasm to develop into over-optimism. That was almost eighteen months ago now.

In those days there had hardly been time to dwell on the failure. One of our busiest times of the year had fallen on us straight after that cycle: spring crutching, then shearing, with all its attendant preparations including weaning all lambs and moving many mobs of sheep.

My imaginings of life with a baby had ceased abruptly in those days. It had not been dreams of pregnancy that I had mourned, but the special individuals who had been created. Pregnancy was not a necessity for my happiness. I had returned to old thought patterns: work, my interests, the farm program for the coming months. I felt amazed that I had been able to neglect all those things, and that my mind had become so centred on having a baby.

I'd always viewed my life in the same way that I viewed

my garden: it was large, but finite, and into its every nook and cranny I wanted to cram something precious and flourishing. After the disappointment of the first cycle, at least, that view had returned to me.

Shearing. A great time. My second year of wool classing, that had been. I knew every mob, the conditions they'd been under that year, and how that was likely to affect their wool. I relished the challenge of assessing the wool and calculating output so as to see the completion of a bale coincide with the completion of a mob. No untidy mixed bales, and a sale description that would maximise our chances of a good wool cheque.

But shearing was also a time of intensive and unavoidable contact with people for many days at a time. The loss of the babies wouldn't be so hard to handle if you could hole yourself away until you felt better, then be selective about the people you saw and the types of attitudes with which you came into contact. An impossible luxury. I'd hated the scrutiny of others, and didn't want to have to deal with it again. If we could just stop treatment, now, I'd be that much closer to putting it all in the past.

That first shearing, after the first failure, there'd been one shearer who'd never let up. 'When are you and Lester going to have a kid?' 'Perhaps next year there'll be a kid in the shed.' 'Lester firing blanks all the time, is he?' 'You want to leave that pup alone. That's why you've got no baby: it's taking all your maternal instincts.'

The other workers dismissed him as cheeky, and said he had a reputation for pulling everyone's leg. I'd wished he'd done it to Lester, too, then. Come to think of it, why hadn't he? Because infertility was always assumed to be the woman's problem, and it was of course my duty to produce children for the sake of the farm.

It was so hard to deal with. I couldn't simply laugh it off all the time, or divert this shearer by saying that we didn't want kids, because that in itself would be food for talk. I'd be 'uncaring'. I couldn't resort to sarcasm, because that would be construed as evidence of my bitterness. I couldn't do what I really felt like doing—that is, let rip and tell him to shut up—because then I'd be 'super-sensitive'. If I'd fired him the other shearers would walk out with him. It wasn't so much a matter of caring what anyone thought of me or my life, but of having to handle the evidence that they were thinking something. So I'd had to try and remain light through days of this, all the while thinking: If you only knew what a story I could tell you about our efforts to have a family.

What was it about family, anyway, that made people feel that they could ask you about it all the time? 'Don't you want kids?'—betraying their awareness that as yet you have none. Nobody would dream of asking, 'Don't you want a dream career?' 'Don't you want a bigger house?' 'Don't you want to improve your mind?' Odd.

Dr Connell's letter had arrived around that time. 'I feel pleased with the outcome of your cycle, as you have had ten eggs collected, seven fertilised and four frozen: a good result.'

'Pleased with the outcome!' I'd exclaimed to Lester. 'The outcome is supposed to be pregnancy. Never mind that we're not pregnant, seven embryos were created: as though the whole object of the exercise is surgery and fertilisation, not pregnancy.'

'They don't take account of the human side, do they? The fact that our two embryos died.'

'No.'

'Unless it's deliberate: they don't want you to dwell on it.'

'Could be.'

We had discovered that life was wonderful, though, between cycles. That Christmas had been special. Our first effort at hosting a big family get-together, both sides, and I'd pulled out all stops to cook a traditional meal in four courses. Now that I'd proven I could do it, it could be a Weber and salads meal next time.

I'd tried to explain to the clinic counsellor what it was that we found difficult about IVF. Was it after the first failure that she'd rung me? No, the second – the frozen cycle. A nurse had asked her to ring because I'd been distraught during the embryo transfer.

'Are you one of these women who wake up in the morning and think, What's the point of getting up, I haven't got a baby?' the counsellor asked.

'No!' I had been amazed that such an attitude to life could even exist. 'I've got dozens of projects on the boil, and Lester and I are really enthusiastic about our work and our life. No, it's just that the minute I saw the embryos I loved them, I wanted them, and so now I feel terrible that they have died. I want to be pregnant, but if we never get there I'll come to terms with it and I think Lester will too. But I'll always grieve for the babies we've lost, not for some imaginary ones who haven't even been conceived yet, or that we feel cheated out of.'

From this love for each unique embryo had grown the decision that I would never be able to abort an abnormal foetus. That reminded me of another conversation, with my mother, around the time of our fourth cycle. 'I saw on the news this week that there's a new test you can have done,' Mum had said. 'It's similar to an amniocentesis, but it's done even earlier, so it's not as dangerous. Have you heard of it?'

'Yeah.'

'You don't sound very impressed.'

'Because there's probably no point in me having any of those tests anyway. Even if I do get pregnant, I could never abort a foetus with a problem, so what's the point in finding out?'

'What do you mean?' Mum had looked amazed.

'Look at the way losing embryos after only two weeks has affected me. How on earth would I be after six to eight weeks of getting attached to them?'

'But it's not a case of how it affects you.'

'That's not what I mean. I wouldn't be keeping the baby to save my own sanity, I'd be keeping it because it's an individual and unique and it's what has been given to us, even if it has got some abnormality. That's why I've been so deeply affected when we've lost them—because they're each special, and it feels like we've created life and not given it a real chance. Knowing the babies just didn't take is one thing, but deliberately killing them is another.'

'I just don't understand you, Julia. I could do it. I don't agree with abortion generally, but in these circumstances I do. Medicine these days can save so much suffering, save children being born with terrible deformities.'

'Mum, that's a whole different issue. I do agree with choice in abortion, generally. But I've also been brought to see what an emotional, personal issue it must be. Other women can choose what they like, and I'm sure it's a really difficult awful choice and nobody takes it lightly, but I myself could not choose to do it. Here I am madly trying to get embryos to live. How could I ever kill one, as though I'm saying, "No, thanks, this one isn't good enough"?'

'By not thinking of it as a person.'

'Ah, but that's the whole point. I do now.'

And since that was all I could remember of the conversation, I assumed that Mum must have redirected her attention to the TV. I had been amazed, not at my mother's opinion, but at her willingness to impose it. All these issues were so personal: how could Mum judge my decision? Still, she had the right to express an opinion. That was the trouble. You became so hung up about all this, as though you were the only one on earth going through it, therefore the only one entitled to pass judgment on anything to do with reproduction. But it really was awful when people told you what they would do in your circumstances. Who cares? They're not you and they're not in your circumstances.

I supposed that to be the reason why we'd started steering clear of people, after a while. Which was another awful aspect of IVF, and one with which I was fed up. The effects on our social life. We'd be away for generally two weeks at a time on a cycle, and before that there was a month of drug-taking when I didn't feel well or energetic enough to entertain. Tell a lie: some days I'd feel up to it, but the trouble was that you never knew when those days were going to be. So we went out fairly frequently together, but saw very little of friends. And then, of course, after we returned from a cycle, there'd be a period of recovery, and after that all we wanted to do was re-establish our home life and rediscover each other and our couplehood for a while. So it had been a shock to realise at one stage that it had been four months since we'd last entertained. Which led, of course, to more feelings of guilt and inadequacy, until I'd stopped being hard on myself and realised that I couldn't expect to do everything.

The secrecy issue came into this, as well, and had become a bugbear. There were still many friends and family members who were in ignorance of what we were doing. There was still that fear of intrusion. However, the secrecy now began to seem more of a nuisance than the intrusion would be. I had not expected to have to make so many trips away for IVF, and the frequency of those trips was becoming hard to explain.

And to the normal conversational question, 'What have you two been doing with yourselves?' there was nothing much left to reply, if we couldn't talk about what we actually had been doing. So it had become almost better to avoid conversations.

I had postponed my normal activities, such as the local choral group, partly because I knew that I would have to miss some of their meetings, and partly because, when on a course of stimulant injections, I simply felt too tired and uncomfortable to attend. Naturally I would come across other members of the group from time to time, and to their curious questions as to when I would rejoin, I would have loved to answer: 'We're on IVF and I'll start choir again when it's all resolved one way or another.' But, knowing that the decision about secrecy still stood, I instead mumbled about having to go away for regular medical treatment. How quickly this distanced people! You could see a look come into their eyes as if they were thinking there was 'something funny' about you. Yes, this secrecy business would be one to talk to Lester about, if we did decide to go any further.

IVF had even seemed to chip away at the vestiges of social life that we had made a priority, like going to Liz and Matt's beach place. That had been immediately after the second drug cycle. Liz had often suggested a weekend together at Matt's family's beachhouse, two hours' drive the other side of the city. We'd decided on a date, and I had looked up the duration of my first drug cycle. I'd calculated that the beachhouse visit would fall about a week after embryo transfer, which was ideal. It would provide the 'treat to look forward to' that the clinic urged every couple to build into their waiting weeks. Liz assured me that the weekend would not be at all strenuous—just a case of sitting on the beach reading and chatting, and taking quiet walks. I had been really looking forward to it. I felt sure that everything would work out, as the week between transfer and the beach visit provided some leeway in case this cycle proceeded differently to the first.

Which, of course, it did. My follicles had simply not grown as quickly on that cycle as they had just six months before. I had become increasingly anxious as I'd watched the 'leeway' time being consumed. I'd faced facts and decided that I had better ring Liz and warn her that we may have to arrive late to the beachhouse.

'I think you'd do better to cancel altogether,' Dad had suggested, with Lester backing him up.

'There's no way I'm going to do that, Dad. I hate letting anyone down. Besides, we've been looking forward to this for so long. Liz and Matt have had to book the extended family beachhouse. Our social life has been affected enough as it is.'

'When does it look as though your transfer will be?'

'Pickup may be Tuesday, in which case transfer would be Thursday, or Friday at the latest, and we could still get to the beach Saturday.'

'You're talking about going off there the day after transfer? You should be doing nothing!'

'Liz assures me that's what we will be doing.'

'I think you're mad.' It wasn't like Dad to be so emphatic.

'We don't have to decide yet, anyway. I'll just warn her.'

Liz had sounded understanding, but had asked me if we could possibly drive to the beach on the same day as transfer.

'Nobody really understands what this is like, or how tired I feel,' I complained to Lester when reporting the call.

'If you're that tired then we should forget about the beach.'

'Typical! Turn what I say to your own ends! All I meant was that I hate to let Liz down.'

'Settle down! She'll understand. She wanted kids badly too, remember.'

'But they've gone to so much trouble.'

'I know. We have to decide priorities. But wait and see what day pickup is.'

It had turned out to be Wednesday, and I had then to admit that another sacrifice had to be made. Liz assured me that she and Matt understood completely, but I sensed some disappointment and even annoyance, which added to my embarrassment at having to break an arrangement.

And yet, once I had hung up the phone, an immense feeling of relief had come over me. I had been so very tired, and the thought of doing absolutely nothing felt delightful. The characteristic energy I took for granted was not easily summoned these days, and that weekend of disappointment had been my first realisation that IVF was greedy, a real attention-seeker, and would not leave room for much else.

Lying there in bed, sleepless and indecisive, I felt as though life had been in limbo for the eighteen months that we had now been involved with IVF.

Who had it been who had told us about the blastocyst program? Fiona, probably, because she took a national newspaper and she'd read about it. We certainly hadn't heard about it from anyone at our own clinic, which was not offering the technique yet and which in fact now seemed at pains to minimise publicity about it. No, it was Fiona. She'd been so enthusiastic.

'Have you heard about this?'

'No.'

'It's only interstate. They're growing embryos out longer, in a special culture. I can't follow it entirely but I'll fax you the article.'

'Do they say what the success rates are?'

'The way I read it … they say success is as likely for older women as it is for younger.'

This had interested me, as it was certainly not the case with 'conventional' IVF that older women were as likely to succeed as younger, and I was now in that 'older' age category. I read Fiona's fax as soon as it came. The interstate clinic seemed to be finding out that it was not so much a question of some IVF embryos not implanting, as of them not growing to a sufficient stage to be able to implant. Only some ever grew into blastocysts – multiple-celled embryos – and these, of course, were the best ones to transfer. It made sense.

I did not want to return ad infinitum to the clinic we had been attending. They wouldn't try anything different to help me. Twice out of the four cycles I'd been almost convinced that I was falling pregnant. I suspected that my latter, luteal phase couldn't support the embryo and that I'd had early miscarriages. It was my conviction that a woman of thirty-eight knows her own body and its rhythms like nobody else can, and I had known that implantation had begun. I had experienced all those feelings that I would never have normally: nausea, cramps. And then, four devastating times, that early spotting, as though a period was inevitable. But try telling the doctors that you thought you might be able to contribute some ideas to your own treatment.

We had tried telling them, of course. We'd seen Dr Connell to discuss giving greater support to my luteal phase, but he had dismissed me. Once again, as in his letter, he had given the impression that we had been marvellously successful simply because we had managed so many eggs collected and fertilised. While he'd enthused about this, it had been hard for me to break in and make the point that I wished to make. Eventually I'd tried to describe to him the ways in which my body had veered from its standard course, that I had been sure that a pregnancy was starting, but that it had been cut short by an early period. Was there anything that could be done to avoid this on a future cycle?

'On a drug cycle this early period would not be possible. Your body is made to behave so artificially that you cannot have a period early.' Listening to him reminded me of school biology lectures. 'You could not have felt pregnant so early, anyway, because the amounts of HCG involved would have been too small to have any effect on you that you would have been conscious of. Women only think they feel pregnant at that stage.'

I had been grateful for Lester's support in the presence of this imperious expert. 'Julia was constantly saying to me that she was having strange feelings in her body, quite at odds with the normal course of things. And this was on a frozen cycle – no drugs to affect her.'

'Perhaps she was just feeling what she wanted to. Take it a bit easier next time and try to find something to take her mind off it. Anyway, I wish you luck.'

I still had my diary entry for proof. When the nausea had first begun after that second transfer, and I'd not wanted to excite Lester, I'd picked up my diary and crammed into the Tuesday spot: 'Today I know I'm pregnant, and once it's confirmed and I'm able to tell Lester this will be the proof that I knew.'

If we didn't go interstate, this was the end of the road for us, that was clear. Lester was too old, according to the law, to be the adoptive father of a baby, and there was no way I was going to try surrogacy or donor eggs.

'Why on earth not?' Mum had stopped still in her tracks. The four of us were walking the dogs. 'Lots of women do.'

'I don't care what lots of women do. I would feel too apart from the whole process. I wouldn't feel it was my child.'

'I could bring myself to do it, if I was in your position.'

There was another considerable factor. I was only just beginning to understand my depression, to recognise it and combat it. I remembered sitting outside the GP's surgery in the car after the fourth failure—not all that long ago. I'd made the appointment for one o'clock, over-estimating how long the shopping would take that day, and there was now half an hour to wait. I no longer felt like staying to see the GP. After all, there was nothing really wrong with me. What was I going to tell him? That I felt out of sorts? Couldn't raise any enthusiasm for anything lately? Felt nervous around people? Big deal. While there was probably some old lady with excruciating arthritis waiting to see him, or a kid with a gash over his eye.

So I'd argued with myself, wondering whether to make some excuse to cancel, go home and use the time more profitably. I could have the ironing done in no time. But something had made me keep the appointment. And when the doctor had asked what he could do for me I'd said: 'I don't know if you can do anything for me because I don't know if I've got a medical problem.' My voice had started to shake. He'd said, 'You let me be the judge of that.' And all of a sudden I'd been sobbing uncontrollably, shaking, coughing, apologising. I felt so relieved not to be pretending any more. So relieved to say how miserable, puzzled, frustrated and tired I felt. How I couldn't understand why I was scared of people all of a sudden, why I couldn't think any positive thoughts. Negative ideas were constantly appearing in my head, like obnoxious hecklers pushing to the front of a crowd.

One factor I had not been able to articulate at that stage was that a hitherto unquestionable formula—that results are proportionate to effort – had been relegated to my mental rubbish bin.

The doctor had handed me a piece of paper and a pen. 'List for me all the significant events in your life over the last five years. Include losing ten babies.' I'd cried again, and written. Marriage, change of work, moving house, major surgery ... it was a long list. And I'd seen immediately that it was time to stop trying to cope brilliantly, and eliminate superfluous demands from my life.

The doctor had then told me that I was suffering from a clinical level of depression, hopefully temporary, brought on by IVF in conjunction with other major recent changes in my life. He perceived that my self-esteem was at an extremely low point, after months of focusing on failure, guilt and grief. He hadn't wanted to prescribe anti-depressant drugs because of the effect they could have on the success of future IVF cycles. Instead he'd wanted me to spend a few sessions with a counsellor, working towards understanding my thought patterns and feelings.

This I'd done. I'd invested an hour once a fortnight, and a few minutes each day of related reading, in myself and my emotional health. And it was just beginning to work. Had it worked to the point where I felt strong enough to try again? Would I recognise the beginnings of depression in myself, on a cycle, and act to fight it?

The depression didn't disappear in a steady fashion, of course. It came and went with events. Inadvertent comments, an ad showing kids, Mother's Day, they could all bring it back. Lester had been great, encouraging me to seek help from books and professionals and allowing me to recover slowly and to have 'off' days. That said, there were times when he'd had enough of my moods, I could tell. I'd even seen that funny male smirk on his face, the one that comes when a man thinks he knows exactly how an emotional female will react. Something is about to upset her, and he knows it, but he just can't be emotional himself at the time, and he struggles to look serious. I'd seen it on other men but never on Lester, not before now.

Whenever we learned of the failure of a cycle, he seemed to overcome it in no time. He'd just carry on working really hard, and soon start talking about the next cycle. Of course, it was a case of having to work really hard. But he never had anything much to say about how he was feeling, unless I drew it out of him. Whereas to me the progression of emotions through the whole turbulent experience needed to be grasped, made permanent and then put behind me, by sharing it in conversation with my partner.

I hated to think what it had all cost, if I was going to take into account all the extras: the cost of going to town, wages for help on the farm. No wonder the clinic made you pay up front, before the cycle. You'd never want to pay afterwards. And yet even with the up-front payment for the drugs, so many bills came in after the cycle: hospital, specialist, anaesthetist, assistant, lab storage, with all the attendant confusion over what was claimable on Medicare and what was not. I begrudged them all, and begrudged every item of mail that reminded us of the waste.

Some women continued for ten or a dozen drug cycles, I knew, but that was up to them. Some only had to take one round of drugs before falling pregnant, and most were between the two extremes and would use up their six funded drug cycles if they had to before deciding to stop.

I didn't want to take any more drugs and I didn't want the government to tell me that six was an acceptable number of drug cycles. With only two drug cycles so far and two frozen, my body had already been vastly affected. My monthly cycles were now quite unpredictable. Intuition told me that the drugs were putting my body under pressure, ageing it. The medicos were full of assurances that there was no link between the IVF drugs and any cancers, but who was to know what the long-term effects would be? I reached over my pillow until my fingertips touched the wooden bedhead. I wanted a long life, and still had a lengthy list of countries left to see, much to learn, much to try.

At the shed, workers were in for autumn crutching. A female shedhand, extremely friendly, bordering on over-inquisitive. Did you take questions as friendliness, or keep your guard up? 'Have you got kids? Yes, of course you must by now. No? Well, you lucky girl.' And for the rest of the three days she must have raised the topic of children, hers or other people's, at least once in an hour.

'Yes! I have had kids—lots of them! They were con-ceived with love and extreme effort and planning; not, like so many, as the result of an accident. I've loved every one of them, and desperately wanted them to come to me so that I could show them all the things I value. They just never grew big enough.' That's what I'd wanted to say, anyway. I'd said it in my mind, at home, after the workers had gone.

It was probably time to stop all this. My thoughts used to glow, charged positive.

It had been a long enough turn on the rollercoaster. I'd been looping the loop, thrown this way and that, my thoughts rendered topsy-turvy. But if we stopped we would walk away from every remaining chance of a thrill. We'd be turning back, when the land of our vision might be just over the next hill. Or it might not.

That little figure in pyjamas, coming into the lounge wanting one last cuddle.

Would it be a boy or a girl? Would she be shy, like her Mum? I could help her over that, understanding it, recognising it. Would he be a lover of animals? He'd have to be, with both parents that way. One sure bet, he'd be determined.

We could go interstate and make inquiries. There was no need to actually commit to any more treatment. I rolled over, snuggled into Lester, and slept.

Chapter Fifteen

I assessed the clinic waiting room in one cool glance. Because it was interstate, and serving a much larger population, I'd had a mental picture that it would be bigger.

But it was busy. There were odd single chairs here and there, but nowhere two together for Lester and I. To my right were two vacant chairs separated by one occupied by a young woman. Nothing pretentious about her, no make-up, no status symbol clothes. Glancing up, she realised that Lester and I were together, and moved one seat to the right.

'Thanks,' I said. Then I immediately averted my eyes and opened my handbag. I had noticed the woman's friendly smile and had a horrible feeling that smiling back would be taken as an invitation to start up a conversation. I didn't feel like talking. I didn't know what I felt like doing. I didn't even know if I wanted to be there.

But it was important to keep an open mind for these initial appointments. There was a compulsory session with a counsellor that day. This was the interstate clinic's substitute for an information evening.

The appointment was for nine that morning followed by an appointment with the new specialist at ten. I knew that the idea of a whole hour with a counsellor would create dread in Lester, who was not accustomed to talking to a perfect stranger about emotions and who never felt that he needed help with personal matters. I anticipated the meeting more receptively but even I was surprised at how it proceeded. I had expected the counsellor to immediately ask about our infertility experiences so far and about our resultant feelings. But instead she began by talking about the doctor that we were due to see, about the new technique that he was using, about the way that many patients were 'defecting' to him, and about how thorough and painstaking he was. These recommendations made us feel quite positive and we looked forward to meeting the doctor.

The counsellor encouraged us, knowing that we had already been through IVF and did not need the usual preparation, to use the session in a practical way. She pointed out differences between this clinic and the one we had been using, and dealt with organisational matters to do with the fact that we were coming not only from interstate but from a country area. Many of my fears were allayed and I was very glad of the session.

The counsellor eventually turned to the emotional aspects of infertility treatment. 'You seem very determined,' she said, 'coming all the way over here. Does this positive attitude mean that you've never felt like giving up?'

'Not at all!' I exclaimed, after a quick and astonished glance at Lester. 'I feel slightly better now that a few months have passed since our last failure, but I have to say that I don't feel sure about keeping on going.'

Lester didn't have a chance to put his point of view before the counsellor replied. 'I'm not at all surprised. People don't realise that you go through grief in IVF – definitely so. I read somewhere recently that there are two sorts of grief. There's the sort where someone dies – and when someone dies on you they only do it once! And then there's this sort – chronic or recurring grief, which you have to deal with over and over again. And what's worse, you can't really think of anything that you've actually lost.' She nodded several times in succession, anxious that her point should come across.

'Yes!' I felt so pleased to be understood and to be told that it was okay to feel that grief.

'It's very hard to know when to stop, but I think that you've done the right thing in trying our program because, without wanting to make you any promises, there's a good chance that it may work for you. You'll find with Dr Flett that it'll be clear when to stop because he'll tell you. He doesn't beat about the bush, which some people resent.'

'We won't. We'll appreciate honesty, instead of being encouraged to keep going for the sake of it,' Lester said.

'Have you seen a picture of a blastocyst, by the way? I think I've got some here.' She lifted sheets of paper from a tray on her desk 'Yes, you can have this one.'

She presented us with a picture of a tiny, round embryo with a protrusion on one side, and with many more cell divisions than we had been used to seeing.

'Do we still get to see the embryos before they're put in?' I asked.

'Yes you do.' She told us that they could also be frozen quite successfully.

127

So Lester's first encounter with a counsellor was not too traumatic. The new doctor, too, impressed us. He certainly did not beat about the bush, wasting no time on preliminary chit-chat. He didn't examine me, but it was obvious from the way he talked that he had read my medical history. He launched into a description of the new program and of what he felt that he could do for us. He wanted to increase my dose of HMG, in fact to double it, so as to maximise the number of blastocysts grown on each cycle. He listened intently to my description of the early spotting that worried me so much and had a number of suggestions as to how it could be dealt with. He wanted to investigate why my embryos were not embedding and, again, had various methods of attack at hand. After each cycle, he said, he would meet with us and discuss changes that could be made.

He said that by now my eggs were possibly ageing, and that we might be able to consider donor eggs in that event. I still did not feel that I could do this, and said so. My reasons remained personal, nothing to do with ethical issues of the child's possible half-siblings, or relationship with its biological mother, and everything to do with my need to feel a full connection to the child. But I was saved from going into this by the fact that the doctor merely replied, 'Fine.'

The more we listened the more impressed we were. 'Now, darling,' the doctor continued, 'when did you want to begin?'

I fought back a little grin. I generally objected to 'dear' or 'love' from male strangers, but 'darling' had taken me unawares. 'We want to be over here early in the new year ...'

Lester interrupted. 'It's a very busy time on the farm

between now and Christmas, otherwise we'd try and fit it in before then.'

'Fair enough. I'm going to give you a script for your down-regulation, which you begin after your December period. At that time ring the clinic here and you'll be given all your instructions and your other drugs will be sent over. All clear?'

'Yes.' I scribbled details in my diary.

'I have several forms for you. Your consent forms—we're famous for our many-faceted consent forms. Bring them back with you in January. Blood test requests for both of you, today. Julia, ultrasound for you, today. Lester, sperm analysis for you, today. You'll need to go to our other branch for that, okay?'

'Okay.'

'So I'll see you early next year. Good luck.' We all shook hands.

And so we decided to keep going.

Chapter Sixteen

The interstate appointments had been bearable and we'd committed ourselves to becoming patients there. But, that commitment made, I wanted to postpone acting on it for a while, and even wanted to put it out of my mind. I needed a long break before another cycle, a change – we'd been cheated out of so much and now I wanted to enjoy afresh some of the ordinary pleasures of life. I needed to be able to choose who saw and touched my body. I would stay away from all health practitioners until the next cycle.

We finally set aside some time to visit Liz and Matt's family beachhouse. We loved the setting as soon as we arrived that summer. Brightly coloured shacks faced a cosy bay like toy buildings around a miniature circle of railway, and all doors opened directly onto the beach. No fences, no barriers to communal casual living.

We found Matt and David outside eating icecreams and preparing fishing lines. Matt's 'hello!' was followed by a robust handshake for both of us, but David hardly glanced our way. He wanted to fish, now, but was at least prepared to grab Murray for a squashy hug.

Liz emerged. 'Hi. Just finishing James' iceblock that he absolutely had to have and then decided didn't taste right.'

'Hi. This spot is *perfect*!'

'We like it here. We'd come every weekend of we could, but we have to share it with the rest of the family.'

'You did say it was okay to bring the dog, didn't you?'

'The boys would never have forgiven you if you hadn't.'

As soon as Lester had unloaded the car and changed, I lost him to a boat, a fishing rod and the rare pleasure of male company. Liz and I made green tea and sat on the veranda facing the water. Having reported to one another on the food that we had each brought, and roughly planned a few meals, we were free for news updates. She asked me what we'd been doing.

'We've started looking at house designs, mainly of trans-portable homes.'

'You're not leaving the farm?'

'No!'

'I'm glad of that. James said to me the other day that he enjoys his trips there so much he hopes you don't move until he's at least twelve! So what's the house for?'

'We might put it on a block of land at the coast for a weekend getaway. A bit like the set-up you've got here.'

'Fantastic!'

'Lester's always wanted a beach shack and I'm all for it provided it doesn't replace travelling to new areas. But it would be so easy to spend a few days at a time there over the summer and be able to get home to check windmills. You know, take turns doing that.'

'Uh-huh. You're lucky the farm is near the coast. A lot of farmers wouldn't even be able to contemplate doing this.'

'I know. And meanwhile the planning of it will be a goal to focus on and enjoy instead of IVF.'

Liz had long ago expressed her sympathy over our last attempt, by telephone and in a note that grieved with us and acknowledged that we had endured a loss of something loved, not just a failure of something attempted. I'd appreciated that greatly, but now I appreciated just as much the fact that she didn't express her sympathy again.

'Yes,' she mused. 'That would do you a great deal of good, I think. Both from the point of view of relaxation and a reward for your efforts, and it might take your minds off treatment to the extent that the next cycle works.'

I didn't have great faith in that theory and didn't know what to reply, so I stayed silent and bent to caress Murray.

'You are going to have another try, aren't you?' Liz asked.

'Yes, probably.' I told her a little about the new program and she listened but kept one eye on the water.

'Look!' she interrupted. 'James is rowing!' She stood and pointed to where two men and two boys were waving from an aluminium dinghy a hundred metres offshore. 'He's never rowed before. I'll get a picture.' A camera sat on the plastic outdoor table in front of us and as she readied it she moved forward to the edge of the veranda, into the sunshine, to take the shot. I waved to Lester and then turned my attention to Murray.

'Are you going to have a swim when I've finished my drink?' I asked him, lifting his front paws to my knee. 'Will you go for a swim in the sea?'

Liz turned. I looked up at her, feeling content, and caught a look of pity: to her I was speaking the way I should only speak to a child. It irritated me. Nothing is so irritating to me as people getting me wrong. My ego raises its hackles. You know I've always talked to him like that, I thought. You know it's nothing to do with needing a baby replacement. I wanted to remind her that fudgy dog-talk was a family vice ingrained since my early teens.

'So,' she said, sitting down, 'this new program interstate works better. Why?' I gave her a summary of the principles of the new technique, and she sipped her tea. 'How long do they grow them for?' she asked.

'Up to six days.'

'Why not grow them even longer?'

'Law.'

'What do you mean?'

'The government there has decided that an embryo any older than six days can't be handled, stored, destroyed, whatever.'

'How did they decide that? What's the difference between six, seven or eight days?'

'I don't know, do I?'

Liz slowly brushed sand from the table with her fingertips. Someone must have put bathers or a beach toy there. 'If they don't all grow, you probably won't end up with as many to use, will you?'

'No, but the doctor will probably try to make up for that by stimulating me with a higher dose of drugs.'

'Eek. How do you feel about that?'

'Not really good. That's the main reason why I know I can't stay on this rigmarole forever. That's always been the aspect of IVF that's worried me most, and I wish I could compensate for it with some other sort of medical treatment. But you know that Lester and I are already incredibly careful about our health.'

'What – you think that gives you some honour points to use up doing unhealthy things?'

'No! It makes me want to succeed and stop soon, so we can enjoy being well. I know of women who have an amazingly high number of drug cycles on really heavy doses of drugs, trying and trying. I don't want to get like that. There's more to life.'

'It's getting chilly now, don't you think? Shall we go in?'

'Or walk?'

'All right. We'll walk.' Murray had heard the word and was first down the steps to the sand.

We strolled, breeze-blown, negotiating here an upturned dinghy, there a bottoms-up group of children digging a moat. Like fingers walking, little waves tickled the sand.

Liz tentatively asked how much each cycle was costing us.

'It depends if you mean the whole cost – travel, food, hospital, the farm. Or just the fee payable – nine hundred dollars a time.'

'What would it be without the Medicare help?'

'I'm not really sure, but I have a feeling it's in the order of six or seven thousand. I've read that couples in the UK and USA pay the equivalent of that.'

'Bloody hell. So the government is paying for that each time?'

'Yup! And I'm not even really sick!' I'd often pondered, lately, whether the money spent on IVF would be better spent on areas of medicine that could prevent the loss of actual lives, rather than focusing on potential life. The higher the cost of our turn at IVF, the more I thought about what that money, both ours and the government's, could have achieved when it had so far achieved nothing. I grew to understand, too, that only the relatively affluent would ever pursue IVF to any length, despite the government help.

'I'll tell you one thing that your experience has shown me,' Liz said.

'What's that?'

'That the image that the media gives us is of IVF being a constant success story. And it's not!'

I appreciated her realisation of this. 'That's partly why we went in with such high hopes. The media only ever report the successes, and those who try and try and never succeed are simply forgotten.' Even as I spoke I knew that it would be unfair not to qualify this statement. 'IVF is wonderful, though,' I continued. 'I've been making enquiries about a support group. The woman I rang has just got pregnant with twins after umpteen tries, and she says she'd never known a feeling like it.'

'How fantastic for her,' Liz replied. 'How did it make you feel?'

I laughed wryly. 'Part of me was put out, to tell you the truth. I had quite irrational thoughts like, I'm not joining your group—you're not supposed to get pregnant—you're supposed to support me until I do!'

Liz smiled.

'But really, you have to be pleased for people.'

'Will she stop going to the group now that she's pregnant?' Liz asked.

'No. apparently about half the group have "made it" now, and they still go along and take their babies.'

'Wow. So IVF pregnancies do happen?'

'Definitely. They happen a lot. That's what keeps the rest of us going. By the way, how are Tricia's twins coming along?'

'How did you know about them?'

'You told me!'

'Oh, did I?' She looked surprised. 'Okay.'

I looked at her, waiting for details, but they were obviously not forthcoming. Was I being excluded, protected from 'normal' women's experience in case I could not handle it?

'Auntie Julia!'

'Jamie! You've caught up!'

'Uh-huh.'

'How are you?'

'All right. Can I hold Murray's lead?'

'If you don't pull him. And we'll loose him once we're past the shacks. Did Uncle Lester have a row?'

'Yeah. He was pretty good. Faster than Dad.'

Liz stretched out a hand to ruffle James' hair. The three of us walked a little further before returning to the shack, where by now Lester and Matt were fishing from the beach. The tide had risen some metres even in the short time that we'd been there. Lester was standing behind David, helping him to hold a rod that was too big for him, making him look as though he was about to pole-vault into the water.

'Have you caught my tea?' I asked Lester.

'Sure have.'

I didn't believe him but I looked in the bucket beside him and saw a thirty-centimetre long fish.

'It's a tommy ruff,' James explained.

'You can't be going to keep that?' I said to Lester. 'Put it back.'

'No way.'

'I can't watch this. I'll go in, I think.'

The shack was homey and I spent a few minutes examining the photographs that crowded the walls: family groups tiered on the veranda steps, bold pelicans, the shack threatened by a king tide. Then I started to prepare vegetables and meats for the barbecue.

James was first to return. 'Auntie Julia, will you please play Trouble with me?'

'Yes, all right, when I've finished here. You set it up.' What was I letting myself in for? Was that the game where you had to be a contortionist, and a fit one at that? No, that was Twister.

'I'm ready, are you?' He'd even placed his lollies on the table.

'No. Be patient.'

'I'll take over if you like,' Liz said as she shut the door behind her, came over to the kitchen area and took the peeler from my hands.

James insisted on four games of Trouble, a sort of three-dimensional Ludo. By this time David had come in, and after announcing that there were three tommy ruffs for tea (presumably we wouldn't need the three kilos of meat that were waiting to be cooked) asked if he could play.

'Okay,' I said. 'What colour?'

'NO!' James screamed.

'What do you mean—no?'

'I don't *want* David to play. I want to play with you on my *own*. I never get to play with anyone on my *own*. He

JULIA MASTERS

always comes along.' James was red in the face from anger and frustration.

'You have a choice, James. We invite David to play and we play happily, or we pack it up. I don't want to play with someone who argues and keeps other people out, and anyway you've had four games on your own.'

'Pack it up, then.'

Liz clicked her tongue as the boys ran crying from the room. 'Thanks for not just handing the situation over to me,' she said. 'I have enough of the fights every day. You handled it well.'

'Really? That's all right.'

'Does it make you grateful you haven't got any?'

'Nope!' I laughed.

'Sorry. I shouldn't have said that.'

'Oh, Liz, don't get careful with me. I get this from other people, I'd hate to get it from you, too.'

'What do you mean – "careful"?'

'Bad word, I know. I just don't want you to avoid saying stuff you'd say to people with children.'

She stopped chopping and looked at me. 'Hm. Okay.'

And I knew it would be fine. We couldn't ignore that the world had children in it. I didn't mind the fact that other people had children. I didn't think of myself primarily as childless, or mind still being childless, I only ever minded the children that we had lost. Would others not grasp that? Were they going to pussyfoot around us and guard us from every child that ever was? I was always unprepared for this manifestation of others' view of us, and today, with a close friend, had been the only occasion when I had ever felt able to comment on it.

Over tea Liz said to Matt that we were thinking of building a beachhouse.

'I know,' he said, chewing. 'Lester was telling me, and I've booked us in for this time next year.'

'Great,' I said.

'Hope the roof is actually on by then,' Lester added. 'You might have to bring a couple of tarps to go over your rooms.'

'How many bedrooms will you have?' Matt asked, and nobody, thank goodness, showed any signs of relating the question to that of whether or not we would have children.

'Three,' Lester replied. 'We can always set up more beds in the living area if there's a crowd.'

Later that night I walked Murray along the track behind the shacks. The quiet of the night helped me to pinpoint some feelings. Liz and Matt's understanding contrasted so sharply with behaviour that I had detected in other people. By others, I was being treated as a sad woman, pitied for my difference. And who likes pity? True, IVF was wearing me down. True, I grieved over our losses. True, that state of limbo was a difficult one to be in. But to say that these things were going to dominate my life was false. I loved life, would love it with or without children.

I was glad to have realised this. Having told it to myself, I suddenly lost the need to communicate it to anyone else. I would live with joy when this was past and if I was still childless, I would not let that be my defining aspect. Meanwhile, let what would happen. I'd do my best, but I no longer felt that I could control the outcome of our efforts. This question would, it seemed, be decided for us.

Chapter Seventeen

When we began infertility treatment Lester and I were of one mind. But our attitudes had gradually diverged as I lost my enthusiasm for treatment before he did. This was most marked at the stage when we were at home preparing for our first treatment cycle interstate.

One particular day I was in our regional town, shopping and having a blood test taken. I was also there to collect the stimulant drugs that had been sent by courier to the local hospital. They needed to be kept cold and could be immediately refrigerated at the hospital, whereas they couldn't at our local post office. If all was well I would begin the course of injections in three days' time, and we would be leaving for the new clinic about nine days after that.

Lester was all too aware that he had just twelve days in which to spread all the superphosphate, administer a cobalt bullet to the one-and-a-half-year-old ewes, crutch and vaccinate the old girls who were going to be lambed down early and wean the calves. Lester also hoped that he—we—would be able to make it to a weaner cattle sale scheduled for the following week. There may not be another opportunity to buy young steers after the return from the IVF trip interstate.

He was spreading super now. He tipped the tractor bucket gently and steadily, reversing so that the last bucket-load of super fell evenly into the spreader like a sheet being draped over a bed. Straightening the bucket and resting it on the ground, he left one tractor and walked to the one to which the super-spreader was attached. His favourite dog bounded over for a pat, its body a curved smile of welcome.

'No, I'm not taking you home yet, mate,' Lester said. 'One more load for today, and then we'll go home and see if Ladyboss is back. You wait by the ute.'

He reached the paddock where he was spreading and picked up the line where he'd left off when the last load ran out. There was plenty of time to think while driving the tractor and spreader, given that it took about an hour and a half to put a load out. Long, monotonous lines did not demand a great deal of concentration, so the mind would wander. (How many times had he said to me after he'd spent a day behind the wheel of the tractor; 'I was thinking as I was driving today …' and I'd interrupt, 'Oh, no!' in a mock-serious tone, knowing that a pronouncement was about to be made that would generally involve spending money on some new scheme for the farm.)

He managed to spend time planning the next few days and allocating jobs to them, aware that I would not be able to help a great deal once I was on the drugs. He felt that the pressure, therefore, was really on him, but that was how he liked it in a way. Less time to think. One of us had to be strong, and it looked as though it was going to have to be him. If he had to work long hours and keep his mind on the job, then it was so much easier somehow.

The night before he'd worked till dark – thank goodness for daylight saving – to try to reduce the size of the super heap as much as possible, and then after a late meal he'd gone back to the shearing-shed and crutched a hundred or so of the ewes. So far that job and the spreading were on target, but today was much hotter, more like a real February day, and he didn't like running the tractor in the blazing heat. Too easy for a fire to start that way. He'd put this load out, then go back to the house.

He wondered if the blood had been accepted by the courier without any problems. Our local hospital would not send blood samples interstate, so we'd had to make our own arrangements. He thought, I must remember to ask if there is still enough nasal spray. Although it sat on my bedside table as a reminder to take one puff in the morning, one at night, he couldn't remember seeing me pick it up that morning. Funny that different clinics used different drugs for down-regulation. You would think it would be the same anywhere, he mused. Still, a nasal spray meant less injections. But he'd had to remind me a few times to use the spray, when he himself remembered. Strange how different clinics had different contact arrangements, too. This one had sent us a handbook with a chart that spread over six pages, detailing when it was allowable to contact whom about what at which branch of the clinic. By now we'd already infringed the rules twice.

Lester's mind turned to the stock. It was really time to start feeding grain to the sheep and hay to the cows, as the paddock feed was very poor, but they would just have to wait. There was no point getting the stock used to being fed only to leave them for up to two weeks. Then again he might be able to shift a few mobs around before leaving in order to improve conditions for those about to give birth. So many other jobs he should be doing, too. He hadn't greased and oiled windmills the year before, and it looked as though they wouldn't get done this year, either. Not until our return from the city, anyway. Stock work first, maintenance jobs if there was time.

Time. IVF trips seemed to be taking a great deal of that lately. Well, that was just the way it was—a case of having to persevere until we got the result we were looking for. He knew that I didn't see it that way, and that I had agonised over whether or not I felt able to try again. He knew that each lost embryo had its own face in my mind. But to Lester it was a case of putting each failure behind you and persevering. He grieved, but he tried not to show it. He tried not to put any pressure on his cherished wife, but he felt that it was a mistake to give in to sadness. Better not to quit. Better to tackle what has to be done, the same as with any challenge.

He would not think about the possibility that we may never succeed. Not while there was still a chance. He couldn't really put reasons to his urge to be a father. He only knew that he wanted to turn up to watch the colts or junior netball, have a kid riding in the back of the ute, fall over toys in the house. He had always been at his happiest around children. Always, that was, until a partner came along, and he knew a different sort of happiness. Until then he'd always equated marriage with kids, and thought that finding his wife would be the first step in an inevitable progression towards having a family. Now he could see that a relationship might be enough to fill a life. But, on the other hand, the more that relationship overflowed with love, the bigger was the gap left by the inability to see his wife with her child.

His lines were getting wobbly. Said wife would be driving up there checking windmills and wouldn't miss the opportunity to chiack him about doing a poor job. He took a swig of water from the cooler and turned to check the level of the super. A nice little hole was appearing as the granules fell onto the belt. He'd be glad to get home and cool down.

There was surely reason to feel positive about this next cycle. So many aspects of it promised to offer alternatives. But he wished that I was happier about it and happier generally. Julia's depression seems to be under control, he thought, and her moods more level and sensible. But how long had it been since he'd seen uncontrollable fits of laughter from me, the kind where I'd have tears streaming down my face, making no sound at all and struggling to draw breath? I'd never been one to laugh out of mere politeness, and would sit unamused while his family chuckled over some past incident. But let something strike me as funny (it was usually Lester himself) and I'd be off. He longed to see that again. I'd become practical and seemed to be holding myself together until the infertility issue was resolved.

Two years before it had been 'Isn't IVF wonderful? It'll give us a chance that we never would have had if we'd been trying to have a baby in our parents' time.' And recently: 'IVF is cruel. It's awful. Could anyone dream up a worse torture?'

How Lester felt for me, despite wanting to keep going. Not just the injections, tests, drugs and the immense bodily changes, but all the other stresses. Endless waits by the phone, the worry about what could go wrong at each stage of the process, the emotional load. How difficult it was to be sympathetic and comforting and yet to avoid pressuring his wife one way or the other. And above all never to let slip that to him it was simply a case of doing whatever was necessary to make a pregnancy happen.

He turned again to check the level of the super. Nearly all gone: with any luck the load would run out just as he completed this paddock. He caught the glint of sun on glass from the corner of his eye and twisted around to see that John next door was out mustering a mob of sheep. He'll reckon I'm mad putting super out this early, Lester thought. We won't get a decent rain for two months yet. Well, the job'll be done, anyway, plus we get a discount for the early order.

Two more strips, the load was out and the paddock completed. The dog was in the back of the ute before Lester had switched the tractor off, eager to be home and to find a spot of shade.

As Lester approached the house he was pleased to see the car in the garage. The boot lid was up—I hadn't finished unloading the shopping yet. He'd take the rest of it into the house for me and we'd have a cuppa together. He parked the ute by the petrol bowser and wolf-whistled as I came out of the house for another load.

'Cheeky. How've you got on today?'

'Finished the Bridge paddock. So I thought I'd knock off early and set some hoses flooding, do a few odd jobs. Can you check the mills up here?'

'Yes, depending how long it takes me to get the shopping away. This is the last of it but there's your beer and chainsaw in the boot.'

Lester made a cup of tea while I unpacked bags. 'How did the blood test go?' he asked.

'All right. I got it to the courier and they assured me that it would be there in the morning.'

'Good.'

'I went to the library today.'

'Another Joanna Trollope come out, has it?'

'No. I picked up a book on infertility. I stood there for ages reading it and it seems so good that I might photo-copy some pages.'

'Why don't you buy it instead?'

I was slightly taken aback and paused a moment before replying.

'I could, I suppose, if I can track it down. Not the sort of book I've been used to buying though.' I took an armful of tins into the pantry.

'Sit down and have your drink.'

'I'll drink while I put away.' Back and forth I went, a sip of tea taken on each return to the shopping bags. Lester elaborated on his tractor-driving thoughts, his planned schedule for the coming days.

'Don't plan any work for Sunday. There's an IVF lunch. I suppose you've forgotten.'

'I had,' Lester replied. We had joined an IVF support group, and I read their monthly newsletters avidly as soon as they arrived. Lester would find me weeping, or laughing, or taking notes as I read them. I would fold down the corners of pages that I wanted him to read, either because of a description of some new breakthrough, or because of a particularly poignant letter reflecting our own experience. A local branch of this group had formed recently, and Lester and I had met some of the other members for lunch. To his mind, I had come alive that day. He hadn't seen me enjoy a social occasion as much in months, and the other women and I hadn't stopped talking.

Lester had been dreading the lunch, picturing a 'support group' as one where we would all sit around and take turns sharing our feelings. But he'd gone along because he knew how much it meant to me–as, he supposed, had the other three men agreed to go for their wives. As it turned out there had been another farmer there, ensuring the type of conversation Lester enjoyed. But to him it had been worth going just to see the effect on me. The women had shared every detail of their IVF experiences, as though they'd known each other for years. (The restaurant had been almost empty, apart from one astonished elderly couple who talked little and sat, wide-eyed, eavesdropping.) Sad experiences, funny experiences, wry ones. Since then I had been ringing one of the other women from the group regularly, just for a chat.

'Did you take your Synarel this morning?' Lester remembered to ask. Synarel was the nasal spray that was taking the place of Lucrin injections for the down-regulation stage of the cycle. 'I couldn't remember seeing you pick it up this morning.'

'Mm. But don't let me forget tomorrow to ring the clinic for the blood test results. I'm quite slack remembering everything we have to do this time.'

'And tell me again–when do you start the aspirin?'

'Same time as the HMG. I've put them by the needles, to remind me.' Already the interstate clinic had discovered a factor that our first clinic had not. I had, to a mild degree, an antibody that could cause clotting of my blood as an embryo tried to implant. Aspirin would combat this by thinning my blood. As well, the clinic had done extensive testing of both Lester and me to examine our levels of necessary nutrient minerals, and of toxic chemicals, and had advised dietary changes according to the results.

'By the way,' I continued, 'I want you to ring the van hire people tomorrow.' We had no one to stay with interstate, but at least there was a caravan park near the clinic.

'Tricky, isn't it, when we can't give them a definite date when we'll need it.'

'Just explain why we can't be definite, and give them some outside dates. They'll understand. We've told just about everybody else we've come across, and nobody's bitten our heads off. I'll do it if you're too embarrassed. I couldn't care less what anyone thinks anymore.'

'No, I'll tell him. I wasn't fogging you off.'

'*Fobbing*. F-o-b-b-i n-g. Not only have you got the word wrong, you've picked the wrong expression anyway.'

Chapter Eighteen

Trying to minimise the time away, I had my Day Nine scan and blood tests performed close to home, and sent to the clinic. The scan showed lots of large follicles, indicating that the extra high dose of stimulants had created the desired effect. The blood test would pinpoint the perfect day for egg pickup. But the blood did not arrive at its inter-state destination. A fax came from the clinic: 'No blood? But your scan indicated that your pickup should be the day after tomorrow.'

There was no time to grill the courier company about why the blood had not arrived. Time only to make hasty arrangements, and leave – tired, cross and under pressure.

Lester had a cousin who lived en route. They hadn't seen one another in some time, so it seemed only right to pay her a visit. Naturally, she asked what had brought us over.

'We want to have a family, and the only way we can do that is by IVF. We've had several tries at home with no luck, so we're trying the new program over here.'

Although Lester was aware that I was no longer prepared to be coy about IVF, my ability to be suddenly so open about it had the capacity to surprise him. His cousin and her husband also seemed surprised.

'How old are you, Julia?'

'Thirty-eight.'

'You've got a good few years ahead of you yet, you'll get there.'

'We hope so, but it's not that simple. We've used up two out of six of our funded cycles now, plus it takes it out of you, physically and emotionally.'

'Once you've seen the embryos to be implanted you really identify with them,' Lester thought to add. 'It's not easy to keep creating lives when you don't know if they'll ever actually be born.'

'My advice,' said the cousin's husband, 'is to harden yourselves and not get attached to them or think of them as people. They're just chemicals at this stage.'

'It will be a sad day when I do that,' I replied quickly.

I went into egg pickup convinced that we would obtain our highest number of eggs so far, and that this would mean great things for the success of the cycle: more fertilised eggs, more blastocysts, one that would live. I woke from the anaesthetic and looked at my hand, unbelieving: I'd expected about twenty eggs and the number written on my hand was six.

'Is this right?' I asked a nurse. 'Should it be sixteen?'

'No — six eggs for you today.'

'But my scan showed lots of large follicles.'

'I'll see if I can get the doctor to come and see you.'

The doctor who'd performed the retrieval did pass by while I was still in recovery.

'You're puzzled as to your number of eggs, I hear,' she said.

'Yes. I had my scan done near home two days ago and I've never had so many large follicles.'

'Unfortunately, although the follicles were large the eggs within them weren't quite ready. It simply wasn't worth us taking some of them out. If we'd had your blood from Day Nine your levels would have told us that. Perhaps next time you come over here you can come a bit earlier, to make sure that your Day Nine blood test is done here.'

'Right.'

Next time, must do better. Not allow mistakes to happen. Cram our normal life into an even shorter time frame.

A period of six days of waiting for transfer and allowing the embryos to grow was quite a different matter to two days. I actually had time to recover fully from pickup. It wasn't worth going back to the farm and then returning for transfer, so we tried to have a city holiday with all the treats we couldn't have at home: we had pizza delivered (to our little hired caravan), sat at pavement cafés, window-shopped. We couldn't stay all day sitting around in the caravan. It was a nice enough van, but soon began to feel very small, and the park that we were in very suburban. It wasn't as though we were looking out at a beach and palm trees, or mountain scenery. So we went out and about.

It paid to keep our minds elsewhere as much as possible, because only three of our eggs fertilised, and who was to say if any at all would grow to blastocyst stage?

'Two are still alive, Lester.' I hung up the phone.

'Two, that's good.'

It was now five days after pickup.

'Yes. She said to ring again in the morning to confirm transfer, because one is healthy but the other one started to look fragmented and may not make it to morning.'

'Okay. So be it.'

'Can you show us our blastocyst on a screen?' Lester asked at transfer.

'No, unfortunately not,' the embryologist replied. 'I can show you a picture of one similar to yours.'

'No, thanks, we've already seen the pictures,' I cut in. 'How healthy does this one look that's still alive?'

'It's hard to tell. I would have liked to wait another day to see if it would still grow, but that would have taken it to seven days old, which we're not supposed to do, and I suspected that if I did that it might fragment. So it's better that we go ahead today. I'll get it ready.'

I looked, horrified, at Lester and whispered furiously: 'But if it might fragment in the lab it might fragment inside me, too.'

'Calm down. Perhaps not. Perhaps being inside you will help it.'

'I want to hole myself away for the next few days now we're home, Lester. And definitely not plan any socialising near the time of the pregnancy test.'

'Okay.' Whatever I felt that I needed to do to get through the waiting period was going to be acceptable to Lester. He noticed that I had seemed to take no pleasure in the transfer, didn't 'talk' to the baby as I had done every other time. But neither was I depressed. It was as though I had become quite nonchalant about the whole process. My earlier depression had been such a turning point. It had shunted me forward into middle age. Did I have no more capacity for enthusiasm?

Our last night in the caravan he'd put his hand on my stomach and said, 'We want you to live. Stay in your Mum.'

'Don't talk like that!' I had snapped. And because he hadn't replied, I'd sensed in the dark that he was crestfallen, and had added, 'I'm sorry, Lester. But really, I don't want us to get our hopes up. It's really not going to work. Couldn't you read the body language of the embryologist? No excitement at all. She didn't say one word about it being a good blastocyst or anything. It had just survived long enough to be transferred, and that was all.'

Best just to agree, Lester realised. 'Yes, you're probably right. I just got carried away.' But secretly he wished that we could savour the hopefulness, even if it did evaporate. We still had some tries in reserve.

He noticed that the pregnancy book and photographs of embryos did not come off the bookshelf this time. On every other cycle they'd ended up on the lounge coffee table for nightly perusal. He wondered if I was not allowing myself to imagine at all. How difficult he was finding it to keep joking and laughing, trying to stay cheerful, not knowing what was going through my mind. He'd almost prefer the constant baby talk of earlier cycles. Or the days when he'd take all the workload and I'd still complain about my tummy, even though I'd been at home, quiet all day. Now I insisted on working hard, saying, 'What's the point in being careful?'

Waiting. There was nothing else we could do.

153

Chapter Nineteen

We underwent two more IVF cycles interstate.

The logistics of doing so seemed insurmountable. We were even denied the luxury of choice as to when we had treatment, since the blastocyst lab, still in the experimental stages and funded accordingly, could only open during certain months of the year. We had been lucky initially in that those months coincided with our chosen dates for treatment. Now we were going to have to turn up when it was open, and so we were forced to allocate farm work to the months before and after treatment, and not to the times when particular jobs should be done.

Having ewes lamb and cows calve early is not only poor management practice but takes, respectively, five and nine months of forward planning to ensure that rams and bulls have been put out at appropriate dates. We even brought shearing forward and found ourselves, in a wet spring, trying to keep sheep dry enough for the shearers to work on. Lester had had to crutch these sheep—two and a half thousand ewes—in the space of three weeks to be ready for the shearing date.

Through pressure, heavy drug doses and frayed tempers we tried to take the attitude that if we were going to see this through, then we would give it our all. We had learnt so much over the cycles so far, and rather than let it go to waste we would incorporate it all into improvements in our approach. We ceased to think that the emphasis should be mainly on my health, and became aware that accumulated toxins in Lester may have a detrimental effect on the quality of his sperm. We knew that their number and motility were good, but what of the quality of the actual chromosomes inside? Many years of use, albeit careful use, of farm chemicals could have taken their toll. We both went to great lengths to detoxify: for six months before each cycle we abstained from alcohol and caffeine, purified our diet, underwent acupuncture and obtained Chinese medicines, meditated daily, and postponed the use of any farm chemicals. I continued taking aspirin to prevent the clotting of my blood, and requested progesterone pessaries and a new drug, Proluton, to support my luteal phase. I tried to eliminate all stresses and extra demands from my life, not always with success.

On the second drug cycle interstate, the fourth overall, I actually achieved a pregnancy. It lasted for four days. The little embryo that had tried to implant was not able to produce enough HCG to sustain life. I had an early miscarriage.

We coped amazingly well with this failure. We'd had a forewarning of it, because the tone of the announcement to me when I had rung the clinic for the result of my pregnancy test had not been one of congratulation and certainty, but a lukewarm: 'Your HCG levels will need to rise considerably to maintain this pregnancy.'

We had become inured to disappointment. In fact, I surprised myself by how unemotional I was over what anyone would have thought would be the greatest disappointment of all. If anything I took a little heart from the fact that we seemed to be making progress and that the changes we had made had shown results, even if they were short-lived. It gave me incentive for the fifth try.

Later, after our fifth drug cycle, we found ourselves driving to my parents' home. On a long stretch of the journey Lester took a nap while I drove. It gave me a chance to think.

What was life going to be like now that we no longer needed IVF, that we no more had to feel our energy being consumed by it? We had almost become accustomed to the enormous efforts that we had continually to make. I could hardly imagine life without these demands. But I would still look forward to it. Now there would be time for … well, for the things that we had been wanting to do for so long. The year stretched ahead of us, and instead of having to be interrupted by treatment journeys, it would be punctuated only by pleasant special events that could be anticipated happily.

I indulged one more time in imagining telling my parents that we were finally pregnant. Soon I would imagine it no longer.

How would we tell Mum and Dad? It had never really been discussed before. Something like: 'Better get your smocking patterns out, Mum.' Or, perhaps, 'Would you like to help us paint the nursery, Dad?'

No, better not to mess around. 'Mum, Dad, we've something very very special to tell you.' (They'd guess from that much, anyway, but I wasn't going to be cheated out of my full announcement.) 'We're going to have a baby, and you're going to be grandparents again!'

Dad's hand would go straight out to Lester's, while Mum would clutch me in excitement. Then we'd all swap partners. One thing I could picture clearly, and that was their faces—astonished but illuminated. Mum would cry.

I was overwhelmed with a feeling of relief that the whole IVF process was over. It was strange, but the outcome had almost become irrelevant. It didn't matter any more. It was as though we had finally managed to step down from a nightmarish hurdy-gurdy which, until now, had refused to stop and release us. We had stepped back into real life, but the fear and the sickness had left us different people.

I looked at Lester. He was deeply asleep, his seat reclined. He could relax, and sleep, just about anywhere. Then again, he had been driving the big tractor in the dark until all hours, working up a paddock for a crop. Did he share my excitement about the future? He was hardly an open book. Did he have the same hopefulness, the same sense of awakening into a new phase of our lives? Before he had fallen asleep we had been talking about what the next months would hold, and he had told me the he didn't feel the way he had expected to at this point, and that he was only conscious of exhaustion. He didn't know what he wanted any more.

All I had been able to say to him was that he had better get used to the situation. I'd spoken curtly, but I had a refreshing consciousness of being able to move ahead with my life instead of being carried in some out-of-control vehicle, and I didn't want anyone or anything to detract from it.

We stopped in a country town, at a park by a lake, to stretch our legs and let the dog out for a few minutes. As usual these days, I noticed children and babies everywhere—the way they were dressed, how much attention their parents were paying to them. The world seemed overrun by a new generation lately.

The journey soon passed. Mum and Dad had not been told of the visit, and would be more than surprised. They would know that Lester and I had something important to tell them. I was quite sure that my parents would be home, since it was the school holidays (hence all the children in the park, of course) and they avoided taking their caravan away at such times.

Lester drove the final leg of the trip. 'No sign of them being here,' he commented as he pulled into the driveway.

'Yes, there is—the dog's in the window there.' They never left him in alone. There they were in the doorway. Excited greetings all around.

'What brings you up here? We weren't expecting you. Everything all right?'

'Yes. Dad,' I replied. 'It's just that we don't seem to have seen very much of you at all, with all these trips interstate. And with lambing coming up, we'll be tied to the farm for a few months and we won't see much of you then, either, unless you're planning to come down to us. So the work was up to date and we thought we'd drive up and see you. You always say to turn up at any time. Plus we've got something we want to tell you.'

'I see.' Mum didn't think it could be a pregnancy. We had surely not had a chance, since the last cycle, to squeeze in another one. Besides, she could see that we were far too subdued for that to be the news. 'It's lovely to see you. I suppose we're just not that used to unplanned visits from you these days. Cup of tea?'

'Please, Mum.'

'I hope I've got something in the freezer for four.'

'No, don't worry. We'll take you out tonight.'

Mum filled the electric jug at the rainwater tap. 'Did you get the rain we had yesterday?' she asked as she added two cups to the two that sat permanently on the kitchen counter.

'Yes, I took out twenty-six points. I suppose you don't know how heavy it was here?'

'No, but they'll say tonight on the news.'

'You'll have to get a gauge so that we can compare notes.'

'Yes. Here you are. Lounge or sunroom?'

'Here will do.' The cups were passed over the kitchen bar. 'Lester – tea's poured.' He and Dad had been unloading the car.

'So,' Mum asked as we sat down. 'What's this news? Is it good or bad?'

I answered. 'It depends on how you look at it,' I began. 'In fact, now that we're here, I feel a bit silly. We could easily have told you over the phone, it seems to me now, but I suppose we just wanted to give more … definiteness to it.' I took a sip of tea while I pondered whether there existed a better word. 'We've decided to stop IVF, that's all. We just have to accept that we're going to have a childless life.' I'd wondered, earlier, whether to add, 'And we're sorry for the impact that this is going to have on you,' but it seemed redundant, somehow.

'I see,' Mum said, again. She sensed immediately that the freedom that this decision had given us had energised us so that we wanted to mark the occasion or at least get in the car and drive somewhere. 'But you don't surprise us at all — do they, Norman?'

'No. We've wondered how you've managed to keep going this long.'

'It means finality for you, too, of course. You'll never see our child.'

'Frankly, I'd be just as happy to see you two enjoying life again.' Dad's response was quick.

'Julia,' Mum elaborated. 'You haven't taken anything away from us. If you two had a child, that would have given us great joy, but we only wanted it for your sake, not ours. We don't spend our days looking to you to make our lives for us, you know that. So the important thing isn't how we feel, but how you feel. How do you feel?'

'Incredibly relieved.'

'How do you feel, Lester?'

Lester took a moment to answer. 'One part of me would have liked to keep trying, but I guess if it was going to work for us it would have worked by now. And I know that each cycle is taking a physical toll on Julia, let alone each failure making the grief worse for her.'

'Yes.' Mum leant forward, forearms on knees. 'You've been dwelling for nigh on three years now on the lack in your lives. It's bound to wear you down, and your view of yourselves. You two are very blessed. You've given this your best shot, and now I should think it's time to enjoy what else life has to offer, while you still have your health.'

'That's what I intend to do. Value every day. What we

intend to do, though Lester's having a harder time coming to grips with the disappointment.'

'But if you're nothing without a child, what are you?' Mum asked Lester. But he wasn't quite ready to grapple with the logic of that one. It would take a little longer for him, yet, while I had been doing my grieving since a much earlier time.

We waited a while for his response to the rhetorical question. He spoke hesitatingly, with long pauses. 'I'll always feel that we've missed out on something wonderful,' he said, 'but we couldn't have tried harder than we have and I'm proud of that. And we have a wonderful marriage.'

Mum and Dad nodded, and I smiled at Lester, thinking of the early IVF attempts when I'd offered to let him find somebody fertile.

'I'm not going to cry over spilt milk,' he continued. 'We had to do what we had to do. But I would have liked to have a momentum for all our efforts.'

We all ignored the wrongly chosen word at this time when Lester was sharing his feelings with us. What he had left unspoken, of course, was that he would have liked to present his mother with another grandchild.

'I should think you both feel as though you deserve an honorary medical degree by now,' Mum said.

'Actually, a medical degree might be a good thing to have,' Lester said. 'It's the not knowing why we haven't succeeded that's hard. You almost feel as though you ought to keep investigating till you get an answer. Except that you could still be there in ten years' time on IVF, looking for that answer. I'll admit that there are better ways that we could spend those ten years.'

We were all silent.

'Where are you taking us for tea?' Dad asked.

'Up the road?'

'Fine.' Up The Road was the name we had given the nearest pub, which served cheap meals and provided a plentiful salad bar. 'Want to walk the dogs with me, meanwhile, Lester?'

'Too right.'

Mum and I went out into the garden, where I wanted to inspect roses that Mum had grown from cuttings. 'This one's looking good. What is it?'

'That's that peach rose that next door gave me. I'll be able to give you a cutting of it this year.'

'Good.'

'Getting back to what we were talking about before. Knowing what you know now, would you go through it all again if you knew that at some stage it would work?'

'That's an interesting one. I suppose you assume I'll say yes, don't you?'

'Not necessarily.'

'If it was guaranteed to work on one or other of the cycles, yes, I would go through it, even now that my blinkers have been taken off as to just what hard work IVF is. Who wouldn't? But that's the whole issue with IVF, isn't it? You don't know that it's going to work, it's such a big gamble.'

'Of course.' Mum snapped off the dead head of a rose.

'Without that guarantee, though, there's no way I'd go through all I have if I'd known what it was going to be like. It's changed us.'

'Changed your relationship?'

'No, I don't think so. It's the only hardship we've ever

had to go through together and at least we know from it that we'll give each other pretty good support, whatever happens to us. No, it's changed us as individuals. It's changed my view of life. Don't ask me how, now, because I'm not exactly clear other than that it's got to do with feeling that my right to control the pattern of my life is one of the most precious things I have.'

'I could have told you that.'

'Mm. But I just wonder what I've done to my health, my outlook, what I could have done with all that time. What would have happened to all those babies.'

'And Lester?'

I considered. 'He doesn't see the world now as so … benevolent.' But the ultimate acceptance that life, in this regard, could be cruel, would have to come from him. I had done all that I could.

'Yes.'

I dragged a plastic chair into a sunny spot and sat while Mum pottered. The sun would soon disappear behind the suburban houses and fences. 'I think on the last two cycles, it's almost as though we've kept going just because we were angry and frustrated at what we had lost up to that point. We were caught up in it, like gamblers. As though we'd never be able to get back what we've lost. Better to cut our losses.'

'You were addicted to the possibility.'

'Yes, that's putting it well. It was as though having a child wasn't the goal anymore, that we were more interested in making sure that all the effort wasn't wasted.'

'Never forget that you have created the beginnings of life. Your efforts haven't been wasted.'

'Yes, and I'll always wonder what would have happened. Perhaps' — my eyes moistened and my voice became a little softer — 'they'll end up in a rose or a puppy or something nice.'

Mum knew that it was only heartfelt emotion that led to such loss of common sense, and waited. I composed myself. 'I really feel,' I said, 'for all the couples who don't even get as far as we did. Can't produce eggs, or sperm, or the embryos never grow, or whatever. Things seemed to go really well for us at times and I know that for other people it can be even more traumatic. At least we had the joy seven times of seeing our embryos and knowing that they were alive for a few days.' I must be getting better: I could say this dry-eyed, with pride.

'You'll have to deal with people's criticism, you know.'

'What do you mean?'

'People will say heartless, stupid things. Say that you can't really want a child that much if you've stopped IVF before you absolutely have to.'

'They don't realise, do they, what it's really like, how the anxiety invades you and how you can't have a life until it's all over.'

'No, of course not.'

'That is, if you're not amongst the lucky ones who succeed on the first or second try. Anyway, if one positive has come out of this it's that I've learnt to anticipate other people's ignorance and not be bothered by it.'

'Good. And what are your plans?'

'Everything that I've ever wanted to do that I haven't.'

'Even better.'

I knew, though, that there would still be a period of

adjustment. Only a few days earlier, I had found myself making mental note of a pretty name for a girl. It had shocked me to realise that there was no point in doing that any more.

And I would forever miss seeing Lester holding our child, and miss seeing my parents with that child, too.

'Are you sure you're not sad?' I asked again.

Mum looked up. 'I've been sad. When you and Lester first started all this and we were all hopeful, and it came to nothing. Your father and I have gone through it, too.'

'We know.'

'But it's just like you. Over the months the sadness has eased and the scales lean more towards wanting happiness from other sources. We certainly don't want to see you suffer, but I won't try to tell you that there isn't a little part of us feeling vulnerable.'

I nodded. I had wanted this admission that Mum and Dad had been on a similar ride to us, so that I could then hear that they'd come off unscathed.

Two dogs careered excitedly around the corner of the house, followed by two men. I observed Lester. He looked bright as he came towards me.

'What have you and Dad been talking about?' I asked.

'Practical stuff, as we Martians do.'

'What practical stuff?'

Lester looked over to Mum and Dad who, several metres away, were rubbing their dog down with an old towel.

'Your Dad helped me to put a finger on one of the problems I've been worrying about.'

'Oh?'

'Old age. What will our old age be like, if we've got no

kids? Who's going to look after us? Dad asked me if that was something that bothered me and, yes, I've always assumed that would be one of the good parts about having kids.'

'Goodness. I never think of these things. What solutions did you and Dad come up with?'

'None really. But it felt good to realise that it had been at the back of my mind. I guess you and I can think about it as the years go on. You're younger than me, you can push my wheelchair. Anyway, how's my girl?'

'Hungry,' I said, as Mum and Dad joined us.

'Yes, we'd better get ready to take your parents out. The afternoon is rapidly closing to a draw.' I observed him again. No, he hadn't been making a joke. It would be too harsh to laugh at him now, but really, how did he manage to mix his expressions up in quite the way that he did? That was the man that I'd married all right.

I sniggered, it developed into laughter, and Mum was infected too. Dad feigned horror. 'You cheeky things.'

Lester stood enjoying the scene as I fought for breath. That was the girl he'd married.

Girl? I'd be forty next year. Which reminded him of one expression, at least, that he knew perfectly well. The one about life beginning.

Epilogue

Since the writing of this book some IVF clinics have opened satellite branches in country towns, making the experience of country patients somewhat easier.

My purpose in writing *The Rollercoaster* was to reflect the experience not only of country IVF patients, but of all those who finish treatment as childless as when they began it. These people number far more than we had ever imagined, or, I suspect, than most beginning IVF patients ever imagine. IVF is a wonderful development and the joy that it has given is an undeniable achievement. We are not bitter that we could not share in its success but we will always be puzzled that our experience did not accord with the impressions of IVF that we had somehow acquired even before we began treatment. In the celebrations over miracle births those who have not given birth are somehow forgotten, as is the fact that they have often technically conceived and briefly been 'parents'.

Now our grief over our lost babies is still with us, but as with any grief it can eventually be put away in a tiny drawer, like a precious old lace handkerchief, always there but rarely taken out.

Our lives are too full, and will be all too short, for us to allow unhappiness a long audience.

WAKEFIELD PRESS

Harm

Stephanie Luke

'Everyone knows about me. They come to the cinema pretending to purchase tickets, but really it's to see the girl who lives with her insides on display.'

Anna is blessed. She can hear promises pulsing through overhead wires, read invitations in car number-plates, tune in the radio to music from other realms. The pigeons are there to guide her home, even after she's been living three days furiously on air. Touched at last by the hand of God, Anna is ready to make her grand debut.

Unfortunately there are other names for Anna's 'revelations'. Jacob, her delighted workmate who dabbles in DIY psychiatry, prefers the term 'psychotic'. Her girlfriend Sarah, desperate and frightened, finds herelf living with a stranger. While Anna's family plots a rescue dash across the border, the nurses and doctors try to keep her out of harm's way.

As the voices in Anna's head close in, demanding unthinkable sacrifices in exchange for the glory they are offering, she needs to find her place somewhere between the grey world of safety and the luminous one she has glimpsed.

WAKEFIELD PRESS

Someone You Know

Maria Pallotta-Chiarolli

Someone You Know is Maria Pallotta-Chiarolli's biography of Jon, who is living with AIDS, and the story of their extraordinary friendship. Maria and Jon teach together, hold common views; they also share secrets. The threads and entanglements of their lives come together at Jon's final gathering.

'I have rarely been so moved by a piece of writing, in a book or on stage or screen, as I was by the end of *Someone You Know*.' – *Age*

'It's the story of a friendship, of insights into gay life, of a journey that ends in death, but also in birth, in spiritual growth and understanding. It's true, and it's the story of someone you know.' – AIDS Council of South Australia

WAKEFIELD PRESS

Wakefield Press has been publishing good Australian books for over fifty years. For a catalogue of current and forthcoming titles, or to add your name to our mailing list, send your name and address to

Wakefield Press,
Box 2266, Kent Town, South Australia 5071.
TELEPHONE (08) 8362 8800 FAX (08) 8362 7592
WEB www.wakefieldpress.com.au

Wakefield Press thanks Wirra Wirra Vineyards and
Arts South Australia for their continued support.